Agnieszka Cybal-Michalska / Małgorzata Rosalska

Leadership and Management

Complexity and Determinants in School Space

V&R unipress

Bibliographic information published by the Deutsche Nationalbibliothek
The Deutsche Nationalbibliothek lists this publication in the Deutsche Nationalbibliografie;
detailed bibliographic data are available online: https://dnb.de.

Printed with friendly support of the Adam Mickiewicz University in Poznań, Poland.

© 2025 by Brill | V&R unipress, Robert-Bosch-Breite 10, 37079 Göttingen, Germany, info@v-r.de,
an imprint of the Brill-Group
(Koninklijke Brill BV, Leiden, The Netherlands; Brill USA Inc., Boston MA, USA; Brill Asia Pte Ltd,
Singapore; Brill Deutschland GmbH, Paderborn, Germany; Brill Österreich GmbH, Vienna, Austria)
Koninklijke Brill BV incorporates the imprints Brill, Brill Nijhoff, Brill Schöningh, Brill Fink,
Brill mentis, Brill Wageningen Academic, Vandenhoeck & Ruprecht, Böhlau and V&R unipress.
Unless otherwise stated, this publication is licensed under the Creative Commons License
Attribution-Non Commercial-No Derivatives 4.0 (see https://creativecommons.org/licenses/
by-nc-nd/4.0/) and can be accessed under DOI 10.14220/9783737018555. Any use in cases other
than those permitted by this license requires the prior written permission from the publisher.

Printed and bound by CPI books GmbH, Birkstraße 10, 25917 Leck, Germany
Printed in the EU.

Vandenhoeck & Ruprecht Verlage | www.vandenhoeck-ruprecht-verlage.com

ISBN 978-3-8471-1855-8

Contents

Introduction 7

Agnieszka Cybal-Michalska
Chapter I: Leadership – contexts and theoretical framework 9
1.1 Leadership – definitions and approaches 9
1.2 Leadership theories 14
1.3 Factors, dimensions, functions and types of leadership 15
1.4 Leadership styles and the role of power in leadership 20

Małgorzata Rosalska
Chapter II: Leadership in school communities 27
2.1 Leadership in education 27
2.2 Educational leadership 33
2.3 Principal as a leader 37

Agnieszka Cybal-Michalska
Chapter III: "Management" – selected theoretical approaches 41
3.1 Management – the evolution of the notion and variety of
    definitions 41
3.2 Management theories 42
3.3 Management models and variations 48

Małgorzata Rosalska
Chapter IV: Empowerment as a strategy for management of educational
processes 51
4.1 Empowerment – definitions 52
4.2 Empowerment and management 54
4.3 Empowerment in education 57
4.4 Determinants of the implementation of the empowerment concept
    into educational practice 62

Małgorzata Rosalska
Chapter V: Building relationships with the community as part of school
management 65
   5.1 Social environment of school 66
   5.2 Strategic management 68
   5.3 Building relationships with environment 71
   5.4 Educational marketing 74

Agnieszka Cybal-Michalska
Chapter VI: Leadership versus management – skills accumulation and
integrity 81
   6.1 Leadership versus management – similarities, differences,
      contemporary issues and challenges 81
   6.2 Personality of a manager versus personality of a leader 83

Agnieszka Cybal-Michalska
Final note: Management for leadership? – educational implications . . . 89

Bibliography 97

Summary 103

Introduction

The discourse presented in this work is focused on the subject of leadership and management, as well as relationships between these two. This discourse requires the inclusion of multicontextual changes of the neoliberal world, which make leaders face new requirements. The most important requirements are: the increasing role of leadership, management for leadership, transformational leadership, styles of management and the ability to manage changes, as well as planning, managing and monitoring careers of organization workers. Subjective shading of leadership and management constructs will be clearly stressed in this text. Accumulated values that create management and leadership competence and values that are useful in their creation and development create leadership career capital and management career capital – and perhaps even management for leadership career capital. It means, that capital (which may accrue but also depreciate, as well as it may be exchanged for "fresh" capital) is a concept that reflects, in an individual's mind, a diagnosis and prognosis of accumulated personal resources (important and conditioned in a "leadership" and "management" way) gained in the process of educational, professional, social and cultural experience. There is no doubt, that while analyzing individual paths of development for leadership or management, one should take into account a wide field of conditions and inquire semantic sense that a subject (including a collective subject) gives to reality to interpret and understand past and new conceptualizations and experience, which make up the domain of management and leadership.

Leadership theories both increasingly shape thinking about the management of educational processes and inform everyday educational practices. Discussions on how general assumptions from the fields of management and leadership can be implemented occur at many levels. They are used in the design of global and local educational policies, in the reflection on the role of school and its relationship with the social environment.

Contemporary trends in management and leadership also help design the profile of a school principal, who is prepared to fulfil diverse roles required by the dynamics of modern school. This perspective is crucial in the selection of content presented in this publication. Awareness of the variety of tasks, roles and expectations of a school community leader, formulated by partners in the social environment, is the basis for the selection of topics that most convincingly demonstrate the need for management and leadership knowledge for a school principal and its use in educational practice.

School can be seen as one of the many institutions which, through the efficient management and competence of a principal as a leader, can significantly improve its performance and the results of its actions. In the context of education, however, this perspective appears to be clearly inadequate. A school is not only an organisation, but also a community of learners who are in constant, yet dynamic relationships with one another. It is difficult to interpret educational processes without taking into account the structure and dynamics of the external environment. Hence, in addition to demonstrating selected concepts of education and educational leadership, issues concerning the management of internal and external processes will be addressed in this publication. The chapter devoted to empowerment shows the possibilities of building the school community, strengthening its resources and competences for participation in decision-making, involvement and increasing responsibility. The chapter on building relationships with the social environment aims to identify directions and opportunities for strategic management that will foster the achievement of school objectives, taking into account the characteristics of the environment in which and for which it operates. This arrangement of content is intended not only to identify areas of educational leadership, but also to indicate selected fields of competence that can strengthen the professional resources of a leader in educational processes.

Agnieszka Cybal-Michalska, Małgorzata Rosalska

Agnieszka Cybal-Michalska

Chapter I:
Leadership – contexts and theoretical framework

1.1 Leadership – definitions and approaches

The multicontextual social transformations expressed though the permanent creation of contemporary society, the specificity of qualitatively new changes in the relations between the global and the local, society and subject, organisation and individual, and the interlinks between them, are not insignificant for considerations of leadership concept.

The conceptual complexity of the leadership phenomenon and its aspects, such as: multidimensionality (the correlate of biological, cognitive, behavioural, social factors), multidirectionality (the variety of styles, factors and dimensions), flexibility (the possibility of development in different directions), contextual character (historical, biographical, environmental, situational conditioning of leadership) determine the need to integrate a multitude of approaches and theoretical orientations. In this context, it is fair to risk stating that we are witnessing the integration of micro-theory with meta-theory.

The last four decades have seen a proliferation and multiplicity of co-occurring theoretical assumptions concerning leadership. The value of career theory debate is evidenced by the fact that it is not free from a reinvigorated critical examination of many theoretical perspectives. From the reflections undertaken in this chapter, it is clear that there is a need to generate new approaches that transcend the boundaries defined by fragmentary paradigms so that they are relevant to the dynamics of modern world transformations and the challenges posed to effective leadership.[1]

---

[1] The cognitive findings made are part of the multi-contextual considerations on the area of leadership, which the author included in her diploma thesis written under the supervision of prof. Jacek Sójka, as part of the MBA Higher Education Management studies entitled Leadership and management – their conditions and complexity, Poznań 2014. Moreover, the author also addressed the issue of leadership in the article: Cybal-Michalska Agnieszka, Leadership – reflections on its concepts and their categorization according to the range of existing prop-

It is worth starting the interdisciplinary discourse with the reflections of Warren Bennis, which may be an interesting cognitive contribution to pondering the essence of leadership. Using a very peculiar language, the author stated that he once thought that leading an organisation was equivalent to conducting a symphony orchestra. But "I don't think so anymore; it is more like jazz because there is more improvisation involved in the process" (Sharma & Jain, 2013, p. 309). Thus, demonstrating the difficulty of formulating (and arguably testing) theories about leadership and questions regarding how the essence of leadership manifests itself, become fundamental to the leadership theory and practice.

Pondering over a possible range and classification of theories grouping the approaches to explaining leadership, it is necessary to refer not only to the theoretical background of this phenomenon, but also to its everyday dimension, to the practical sphere referring to biographical contexts and the development of leadership attitudes (or behaviours) in the individual course of life. This discourse is conducted by representatives of various disciplines, in particular: sociologists, political scientists, social psychologists, management science theorists and practitioners. In the literature, various systemisations of the way in which leadership is approached can be identified and, as Michalak puts it, the changes in semantic framing stem from the need for increasingly better recognition of the phenomenon and the quality of the transformations in the external environment faced by organisations and their leaders (Michalak, 2014, pp. 4–5).

When attempting to conceptually define the category of "leadership", it is difficult to overlook the lack of focus and ambiguity in the semantic meanings attributed to the term. Stogdill concluded that there are almost as many definitions of leadership as there are people who have tried to define the concept (Bohoris & Vorria, 2007, p. 1). In the context of the narrative undertaken, it seems justified to use the phrase managerial leadership, since the organisation constitutes an interesting space for reflection. The introduction of the adjective qualifier helps somewhat alleviate the dilemmas with specifying the definitional *credo*. Starting from the definition of managerial leadership as the process of directing and influencing the activities of group members related to the group's tasks (Stoner, Freeman & Gilbert, 2001, pp. 453–454), Stoner, Freeman and Gilbert, identified the aspects with which the leadership domain is intrinsically linked. In doing so, they recognised that leadership is related the following: other people, the unequal distribution of power, the ability to use various forms of power, and values. Particularly interesting (not only cognitively) for practice is the authors' attention to the moral components of leadership (Stoner, Freeman & Gilbert, 2001, p. 454). Maxwell, an American expert on leadership issues, sees

---

ositions, [in:] Sławomir Banaszak/Kazunobu Oyama, Japanese and Polish Managers, 2023, V&R unipress.

ethical threads in leadership as a leader's core empowerment. He regards the foundation of effective leadership as "seeing the value of others – not because they can do something, but simply because they are human beings" (Maxwell, 2010, p. 49). The apparent lack of a unified thought on the subject of approaching leadership means that the scope of the concept can involve its subjective and objective meaning structure, understanding or framing from either the organisational or individual perspective.

Indeed, a distinguishing feature in thinking about leadership is the variety of meanings in which the concept is sometimes used. Although it is difficult to make a complete list, this definitional multiplicity can be reduced to a few basic dimensions of the "leadership" notion, showing what is denoted and connoted by the distinguished conceptual category. Among the various approaches to the ways of defining leadership, following Michalak, four can be distinguished which have acquired a particular theoretical and empirical significance. Thus, leadership can be viewed as: a) a trait (attention is focused on personal characteristics of an individual, fixed personality traits that are linked to leader's character and predisposition. Trait theories assume that there are individuals who have an innate ability to lead others, stand out from the crowd and achieve success. The distinguished theoretical orientation seeks to identify a specific set of personal traits indicative of effective leadership and influence on others); b) skill (attention is focused on leadership skills, the essence of which is the ability to win people over, to involve others in the process of achieving goals, and to lead others. This approach emphasises the importance of leadership skills and the possibility of developing them through accomplishing successive tasks); c) social relationship (the focus is on the relational nature and influence between those leading (leaders) and their followers. The distinguished subjects are treated as important "entities" of the leadership process subordinated to the achievement of the intended goals and perceived from the perspective of the relationship they establish); d) social process (emphasising the processual and relational context of leadership – influencing an individual, a group for the realisation of jointly agreed goals – treated as an orderly sequence of changes, following one another in a specific temporal dynamics. Facts indicative of leadership in the processual sense most often include: having a vision, building a strategy, influencing team members to achieve better results, motivating, setting an example and encouraging cooperation within the team) (Michalak, 2014, pp. 7–9).

From the above, it is clear that the "process", "influence", constitutes the aspect of the leadership "mechanism" that obtains significance. Leadership, as Sharma and Jain frame it, is the process by which an individual exerts influence on others to achieve an intended goal. The leadership subject directs the organisation so that it operates in a more cohesive and coherent way. The authors explicitly refer to Northouse's definition of leadership as a process in which an individual influences a group, for the purpose of achieving a common goal (Sharma & Jain, 2013, p. 310). Michalak speaks in a similar vein about leadership. Focusing on the processual nature of leadership and treating leadership as a complex social process connected with influencing others and gaining followers to achieve goals, the author defines leadership as "a process of influencing others to jointly achieve agreed intentions. Understood in this way, leadership shows that we should associate it with the ability to gain followers rather than with a social function and position" (Michalak, 2014, pp. 9–10).

The category of "leadership", defined as a process in which an individual influences others and does so in order to attain group or organisational goals, according to Grey and Shaik, is further linked to an emphasis on the requirement for this process to have a beneficial impact on both the individual and the organisation. The authors define leadership as a process of social influence (in literature we can also encounter statements that leadership is not different from the processes of social influence occurring among group members), which cannot exist without a leader and followers. This involves volunteering on the part of followers and it modifies their behaviour (Mahmood, Muhammad & Bashir, 2012, p. 513). The view under discussion resonates with Drucker's reflections. His views on leadership are defined by observing the significance of having followers. The author firmly states that the only definition of a leader entails recognising that a leader is simply someone who has followers. Gaining followers and disciples requires influence, but does not preclude a lack of integrity in achieving goals (Bohoris & Vorria, 2007, p. 1).

Jago's inquiries took a similar direction. People become good leaders. A leader is not born. In other words: being a leader is a merit of "becoming" and not fate or chance. As a result, the author states straightforwardly that if you have the desire and willpower, you can become an effective leader. Good leaders are shaped through a never-ending process of self-development, education, training and experience. Good leaders constantly work and learn to improve their leadership skills; they by no means rest on their laurels (Sharma & Jain, 2013, pp. 309–310). At this point, one can venture to say that leadership is everything an individual undertakes to lead effectively (see: Bohoris & Vorria, 2007, p. 1).

The plethora of theoretical attempts to define "leadership" thus, reveals the multiplicity of approaches in the analysis of this complex phenomenon. Contemporary discussion on leadership is largely linked to an emphasis on the proactive behaviour of the subject. A significant contribution to the development of this perspective on leadership comes from the interactional orientation: leadership is a process (processual aspect), where an individual influences a group (structural aspect) to achieve a common goal (functional aspect). Moreover, contemporary attempts to approach the issue of "leadership" holistically show the crystallisation of new paradigmatic resolutions. Key components of leadership include: the processual nature, the link to influencing others, performing in the context of the group, and working towards a goal (Ricketts, 2009, pp. 1–2).

The holistic nature of leadership considerations is reflected in attempts to categorise and group them within leadership characteristics or principles. Diverse perspectives in the way theoretical positions are systematised are presented below.

Understanding leadership requires reference to the characteristics of the phenomenon. Understood in this way, leadership can be described by the following characteristics: effective coaching skills, self-confidence, congruence between what is said and what is done ("do what you say"), creativity, empathetic listening skills, vision, inspiring others, long-term focus, maintaining a balance between the needs of an individual and the needs of a group, awareness of realistic conditions, strong self-esteem, a sense of priority in the moment, service mentality, honesty, technical or contextual expertise, trust, willingness to delegate responsibility, willingness to share the credit (Ricketts, 2009, pp. 1–2).

When considering possible leadership perception through the prism of principles, the following recommendations are mentioned: (a) know yourself and strive for self-improvement (striving for self-improvement means constantly strengthening your assets); (b) be technically proficient (as a leader you need to know your job and know what your employees do); c) be accountable for your actions (seek ways to take your organisation to new levels and when something goes wrong do not blame others but analyse the situation, take corrective action and tackle the next challenge); d) make appropriate and timely decisions (when solving problems, planning or making a decision, use appropriate tools); e) lead by example (be a good role model for your employees); f) know your people and look after their well-being (know human nature and know the importance of genuinely caring for employees); g) keep your employees informed (have the knowledge of how to communicate well not only with your employees but also with seniors and key customers); h) develop a sense of responsibility in your employees (help others develop good character traits that will help them carry out their tasks responsibly); i) make sure that tasks are understood, supervised and carried out (concern with communication is a key issue in this respect) (Sharma & Jain, 2013, p. 312).

Reflections on leadership have also been accused of being too simplistic in their approach to human nature. A counterbalance to traditional views on the leadership domain may be the psychoanalytic concept of leadership (emphasising the importance of what is subconscious but revealed in the subject's behaviour and related to the urge to satisfy unfulfilled needs) or the romantic notion of leadership based on an idealised image of a leader, who is a guide and interpreter of the multiple meanings of the organisation's culture (Stoner, Freeman & Gilbert, 2001, pp. 475–476).

The development of scholarly interest in the issue of leadership has resulted in the multiple interpretations of the term. In essence, a number of researchers have proposed to broaden the conceptual definition of leadership as an innate tendency, a certain state. The contemporary account of leadership calls for inquiries into the development of leadership qualities. Although it is of course difficult to provide a complete enumeration, this definitional multiplicity can be reduced to a few basic dimensions of capturing "leadership", showing what is denoted and connoted by the distinguished conceptual category. The above considerations have outlined the multiplicity of problematic approaches in the analysis of this complex phenomenon.

1.2 Leadership theories

The phenomenon of leadership can be analytically and interpretively approached from different theoretical perspectives with different conceptual assumptions. However, attempts to classify them prove to be difficult in terms of clearly sorting out the multiplicity of positions. The reason for this is to be sought in the impossibility of separating them. Taking into account the temporal dynamics, theoretical approaches inspired one another, resulting in distinguishing universals and specific elements in the theoretical view of the leadership issue, as well as the possibilities of its empirical verification or implications for practice.

The search for causal factors of leadership should be accompanied by a reflection on the activity of the acting subject. In Mintzberg's reflections, we find an unambiguous statement: "one becomes a leader through hard work, not by being anointed" (Mintzberg, 2013, p. 26).

Attempts made to classify leadership theories identify their various types revealing the structural singularity of these theories. In Bass's view, there are three ways of explaining the phenomenon of "becoming" a leader. These are as follows:

(a) trait theories – selected character traits can naturally lead an individual to assume a leadership role. In the systematisation made by Michalak, the time frame of such an approach is clearly emphasised. The years 1900–1945 were associated with the description of the desirable personality traits of a leader and the focus on the individual characteristics of a subject that constitute his or her leadership effectiveness (Michalak, 2014, p. 5);

(b) big events theories – a crisis or other significant biographical event may cause an individual to reveal leadership qualities by adapting or adjusting to a newly created situation;

(c) transformational theories also known as leadership process theories – individuals can choose to become leaders and develop leadership skills (Sharma & Jain, 2013, p. 311). Considering the preceding reflections, it is not surprising that the last of the distinguished theoretical approaches has the most adherents today. As Michalak emphasises, the focus on the relationship between leadership style and organisational culture has resulted in increased theoretical and research efforts studying the phenomenon of transformational leadership, whose potential lies in the proactivity of the subject and his or her influence on the cultural context and environmental change (viewing leadership as a process of social influence). Within these, Michalak states that "great importance has been attributed to the interrelationship between the leader, subordinates and the situation; (…) the effectiveness of leadership depends on variables such as the leader's personality, the leader's values and experience, the superior's expectations and behaviour and characteristics, expectations and behaviour of subordinates, the requirements of the task, and the organisational culture" (Michalak, 2014, pp. 5–6).

The awareness of the difficulty in making a separable classification of leadership theories can be seen in the systematisation made by Michalak. The compilation made by the author provides further classification findings that can be seen as a continuation of the classification established by Bass:

(d) behavioural theories – dominated the discourse in the 1940s. They focused on actions (what a leader actually does and what a leader should do), typical behaviours that are characteristic of leadership and responsible for effective leadership;

(e) situational theories – a theoretical and cognitive scope associated with the breakthrough in leadership research occurring in the 1950s, 1960s and 1970s. Approaching leadership as an interaction between leaders and subordinates, it focused on emphasising the nature of the task and situational factors (variables) (Michalak, 2014, pp. 5–6).

1.3 Factors, dimensions, functions and types of leadership

A general division of leadership theories, intending to capture accurately their specified conceptual scopes, leads to systematizing the theoretical positions according to certain factors, dimensions, functions and types of leadership. Historically, leadership theories have focused on selected variables attributing to them the causal power to manifest leadership qualities in practice.

This opinion is presented by Blanchard and Hersey. The authors made the issue more specific to finally distinguish the following co-existing views on tasks

and relationships. Introducing the category of broader clarification, in which they included additional contexts and problem areas, they focused on discussing the following aspects:
- autocratic – democratic
- authoritarian – egalitarian
- employee-orientation – production-orientation
- focus on achieving goals – focus on maintaining a group
- ability to perform – likability
- instrumentality – expressiveness
- effectiveness – efficiency

Discussions on this topic revealed that the differences appear to be related more to semantic scope than to the actual types of behaviour occurring. It was believed that tasks and relationships as structural components of leader behavioural styles should be presented as one dimension along a continuum, e. g.: from a very authoritarian style (task-focused) to a very democratic style (relationship-focused). However, this idea has been challenged. Research conducted by the Bureau of Business Research at Ohio State University in 1945 questioned the validity of capturing leader behaviour along a single continuum. This research identified the "basic structure", i. e. tasks and relationships, as the two most important aspects of leadership. The notion of "initiating structure" was introduced, referring to the relational component of leader's behaviour, the quality of the relationship between him or her and employees, as well as the issue of fostering organisational development, good communication practice and accepted procedures. No little emphasis was placed on "mindfulness" treated as attentiveness – a quality that characterises the behaviour typical of a friendly relationship based on mutual trust, respect and cordiality between a leader and his or her subordinates. Subsequent studies have shown that it is appropriate to speak rather of certain leadership styles and confirmed the thesis that one cannot speak of a single continuum, but rather of two separate axes. These findings focused on a few segments that are part of an overall possible approach to the issue. As a result, it was highlighted that there are leaders who rigorously organise the task structure of their employees, when others may focus mainly on creating and maintaining good relationships with their employees. This issue has become even more important, as leaders who display both task-oriented and relationship-oriented behaviours have also been distinguished, as well as those who show no interest in organising their employees' tasks or developing interpersonal relationships. In this context, it is worth noting the reflections of Blake and Mouton, who popularised task- and relationship-oriented dimensions of leadership, using an elaborated "leadership grid" presenting five types of leadership (based on concern for production (tasks) and concern for people (relationships)) in programmes dedicated to organisational and managerial development. Halpin spoke in a similar vein about the key aspects of leadership, arguing that effective or desirable leadership behaviour is characterised by high performance, both in terms of "initiating structure" and consideration (Blanchard & Hersey, 1996, p. 44). Similarly to Blake and Mouton, Halpin concluded that the ideal and most desirable leadership style combines two elements: "team management" (maximum concern for production and people). Unsurprisingly – the least desirable style was considered to be the "passive" style exemplifying ignorance of both people and tasks (Blanchard & Hersey, 1996, pp. 42–44). This theme was also reflected upon by Michalak. The author notes that the relationship between a leader and subordinates goes through four stages and is linked to employee development. The leader should be aware of these stages and make changes in leadership styles. Otherwise, he or she will only be effective in selected situations. The trend appears to be as follows: "from being task-oriented, to being task- and relationship-oriented, towards being relationship-oriented only, to being both low task- and relationship oriented" (Michalak, 2014, pp. 13–14).

It is clear from the above that the meanings given to leadership crystallise around dominant messages and are rooted in specific spatial-temporal conditions. They express meanings that have been given to leadership and are therefore typical in the organisational environment and are perceived by participants in the "relational" leadership process. Hence, the scholarly interests of leadership theorists regarding the functions and factors of leadership should be placed naturally in the stream of reflection on understanding leadership.

Leadership functions can be defined as task-related and group-sustaining activities, the performance of which by the leader or by another person is essential to the effective functioning of groups (Stoner, Freeman & Gilbert, 2001, p. 457). The functional component of leadership can be considered through the lens of tasks and the quality of the group structure. Leadership has two basic functions: it contributes to problem solving, task performance and sustaining the group (Stoner, Freeman & Gilbert, 2001, p. 457). Thus, effective leadership can be considered to involve a behavioural-social component.

The authors seek answers to questions about the existence of regularities (responsible factors), according to which it is possible to identify patterns which shape leadership attitudes and behaviours.

When viewing the phenomenon of leadership, which is a process of "becoming", four of its factors can be grasped and distinguished. Sharma and Jain consider "being a leader" as the first of these. The essence is made up of identity threads – knowing who you are, what you know and what you can do. The reflected self is important in this context because how we are perceived in the eyes of others becomes significant. As a result, it is the followers, not the leader, who determine whether the leader is successful. If employees do not trust the leader, he or she will not inspire them and his or her leadership will not be effective. These considerations are accompanied by the recognition that to be successful you need to convince others (not yourself or your superiors), have followers and show that you are worth following (Sharma & Jain, 2013, pp. 310–311). The considerations undertaken are essentially about what is nowadays called transformational leadership or otherwise known as charismatic leadership. Transformational leadership is not limited to the area of transactions (which is a system of exchange, usually of economic or psychological nature, between the leader and subordinates or followers), but goes beyond this realm. The essence is to skilfully influence subordinates and encourage them to follow the leader in order to achieve common goals (e.g. Michalak, 2014, pp. 11–12). Transformational leaders, in Bass's approach, motivate us to do more than we originally intended to do by raising our awareness of the importance and value of the tasks at hand, by leading us beyond our self-interest in favour of the team, the organisation or a more general policy, and by raising our needs to a higher level, i.e. the one of self-actualisation (Stoner, Freeman & Gilbert, 2001, p. 474). Following Hause, we might add that a charismatic leader has an extremely high level of self-confidence, dominance and conviction in the moral rightness of the views he or she professes – or at least the ability to convince his or her followers that he or she has such a belief and conviction (Stoner, Freeman & Gilbert, 2001, p. 457).

A second important element of leadership, linked to the earlier factor, are the "followers". In this context, a good knowledge of one's employees is recommended. Understanding human nature, their needs, emotions, motivations is the key to gaining supporters and, consequently, followers. Psychology of individual differences makes it clear that different leadership styles are a necessity. For example, a newly recruited employee requires more supervision than a more experienced and long-serving person, or the difference in approaches between highly motivated and unmotivated people. "Communication" and, in particular, the quality of communication practice constitutes another important factor for the leadership process. You can recognise that you lead through two-way communication, and this is largely non-verbal communication. "Leading by example" is a clear message that you would not ask someone to do something that you would not do yourself. Both content and form (the way messages are communicated) influence the relationship between the leader and employees. The substantive framework of interest in factors also distinguishes the importance of the "situational context". The permanent change component makes every situation different. What solves one situation will not "work" in another situational context. Therefore, there is a need to respond appropriately to the situation and this means good judgement, choosing the most appropriate action and leadership style. For example, in a situation when you need to talk to your employee about their inappropriate behaviour, confrontation may not have the intended effect at all if it happens too late or too early, is too weak or too forceful (Sharma & Jain, 2013, pp. 310–311). Following Michalak, it can be added that "situational leadership theory emphasises the leader's responsibility to work towards increasing the maturity of subordinates by reducing both the task and relational behaviours of the leader. The leader should demonstrate the ability to set high, but achievable goals for the group and the willingness and ability to work with the group and conduct activities for its development" (Michalak, 2014, pp. 13–14).

What is interesting from a cognitive perspective are the forces that influence the factors highlighted. These include as follows: a) relationships with seniors, b) followers' abilities, c) informal leaders in the organisation, d) the quality of organisation structure. The considerations undertaken and attempts to cognitively approach the issue of leadership factors allow us to conclude that the leadership process theory is more explanatorily precise than the trait theory. In fact, it is the situation that has a greater influence on the actions of a leader than his or her character traits, which, although they may have impressive stability over a long time period, may lose their importance on specific occasions (Sharma & Jain, 2013, pp. 310–311).

In the literature, one can also encounter systemisations of leadership types taking into account selected variables. Kwiatkowski's conceptual considerations referred to the following criteria: power distance and ways of influencing subordinates or followers (emotional and rational leadership), the mode of leader appointment (formal leadership – usually established top-down and informal – established bottom-up; or legal – as a result of socially accepted procedures or traditional – dictated by custom, related to unwritten norms); time (permanent leadership – autocratic and periodic – democratic) (Kwiatkowski, 2011, p. 16, after: Michalak, 2014, p. 11–12)[2].

The cognitive approach to leadership is also focused on identity threads. As proponents of the interactionist perspective emphasise, a career, and therefore a "leadership career" to a large extent depends on "communication processes, understood as negotiating agendas and identity, role and status" (Rokicka, 1992, p. 116). When discussing this aspect of the issue, it is worth specifying that careers and identity are perceived as interconnected aspects and dimensions. Events and interactions in organisational situations lead to changes in defining oneself and others and to behaviours that protect the individual's identity (Blankenship,

---

[2] The distinguished types of leadership were further defined by the author. "Emotional leaders emphasise inspiring extrinsic motivation in team members and meeting their security needs, becoming a 'role model and protective shield' for their followers to change their behaviour. They surround their subordinates with benevolent care. Rational leaders, unlike emotional leaders, emphasise not so much changing behavioural patterns as thinking patterns within the team. Placing importance on the autonomy of team members and their responsibility, they try to influence the team in such a way as to stimulate intrinsic motivation to act".

1973, p. 88). One cannot help but notice evident references to Goffman's "identity politics practised in interactions" (Hałas, 2007, p. 148) in these findings. The changing view of the self "by" others and "with" others is one of the premises of leader's identity development. The emerging leadership Self, at a certain point in time, interacts with the group's influences. It is then that both the subjective Self and the group/team members can notice the changes in them in relation to others. In the early stages of group involvement, individuals are *dependent* on others. Even as they develop their personal efficacy, they rely on others to accomplish tasks. As the individual engages the in the leadership context and assumes the role of a leader, a division into two paths occurs in the group: *a independent path* and *an dependent path*. In the independent path, the subject has aspirations to be a leader and feels motivated to make a difference in the organisation of which he or she is a part. The other members enter the dependent path and become followers (Komives et al., 2005, pp. 604–605).

In summary, one can refer to the phenomenon of leadership through the lens of a leadership career. In the process of career construction, as Savickas emphasises, the essence consists in the development and implementation of professional self-concepts in the professional roles undertaken and performed. Self-concepts are formed through the interaction of the subject's inherent ability to play different roles (including the leadership role, which is interesting for us) and the ability to recognise and evaluate to what extent the role performance meets the approval of others (Patton & McMahon, 2006, p. 63). Therefore, it can be concluded that the realisation of the concept of oneself as a leader in the organisational environment involves a synthesis of knowledge (developed through the quality of playing one's role and by learning from feedback) and the relationship between the leader and social factors.

1.4 Leadership styles and the role of power in leadership

Many authors emphasise the processual-situational and action-related context of leadership. When people consider whether they respect you as a leader, they are not thinking about your attributes, rather they are observing what you do and, thus, get to know who you really are (Sharma & Jain, 2013, p. 311). Indeed, paying attention to what effective leaders do means nothing more than focusing on their leadership styles. Leadership styles can be defined as various behavioural patterns used by leaders when directing and influencing employees (Stoner, Freeman & Gilbert, 2001, p. 457).

The issue of leadership, and thus the consideration of leadership styles, emphasises the practice of maintaining a balance between concern and focus on results and concern and focus on people. In this way, the shaded approach to leadership is reflected in leadership styles. Likert identified two leadership styles. Leaders focus either on results and the tasks that need to be accomplished to achieve these results, or on the people responsible for achieving these results. In contrast, Stogdill, assuming similar dimensions and recognising that they are not necessarily mutually exclusive, identified four leadership styles: a) high concern for both results and people; b) high concern for results and low concern for people; c) low concern for results and high concern for people; d) low concern for both results and people (Kilian, 2007, p. 6).

The above typology undoubtedly inspires further findings. Referring to the "leadership grid" proposed by R. Blake and A. Adams McCanse, one can call the first style above a balanced leadership (if concern for employees and results, tasks is average) or democratic leadership (if concern for employees, results and morale is high), the second can be considered an authoritarian leadership, the third – club leadership, and the fourth – depleted leadership (Stoner, Freeman & Gilbert, 2001, pp. 461–462).

In the light of the above considerations, the findings made by R. Tannenbaum and W. H. Schmidt cannot be ignored. The authors, referring to task-oriented and employee-oriented styles, focused on factors that are responsible for the choice of leadership style. The factors called forces included: forces inherent in the manager, forces inherent in the employees and forces inherent in the situation (Stoner, Freeman & Gilbert, 2001, pp. 457–459).

Research conducted in recent years clearly demonstrates that there is no universal one-size-fits-all leadership style that guarantees success across the board. Different leadership situations require different leadership styles. Moreover, as early as the 1960s, Korman's psychological inquiries pointed to the connection between "initial structure" (tasks) and "mindfulness" (attentiveness to others) and referred to issues of leadership effectiveness, group productivity and performance in stressful situations, absenteeism or turnover. This was confirmed by Fiedler's research. The author concluded that both directive task- and results-oriented leaders and those who are relationship-oriented are successful under certain conditions. Empirical research therefore, does not provide an answer to the existence of the best leadership style. Effective leaders, who have a legitimate track record of success, can adapt their leadership behaviour to the needs of followers and to the specific situation. Effectiveness, therefore, depends on the leader, the followers and the situation. The essence is to diagnose one's behaviour in the light of the specific environment. Thus, the relevant variables of this process include: organisation skills of the leader, superiors, associates and the situation and demand of the environment. Effective leaders have a choice: they have to adjust their leadership styles or change some or all of the variables. Leadership styles are characterized either by behaviours or attitudes. In the latter case, a permanent attitude toward someone or something is emphasised. Accordingly, attitudes carry less flexibility in leadership actions. Generalizing and referring to the evaluative and appraisal components of leadership discussed in earlier subsections, it can be concluded that in organizations, a high degree of concern for both results and people is desirable. But yet, leaders who show such concern are not always able to provide emotional and social support. Taking into account the behavioural component, it can be considered, for example, that if employees are emotionally mature then they are able to take responsibility for themselves. In such a situation, a low level of concern for tasks and relationships may prove to be an appropriate leadership style. Employees form a team and in such cases, the leader allows his or her subordinates to participate in planning, organising and controlling their own activities. By delegating tasks, the leader plays a secondary role and only supports his or her employees when they need it (Blanchard & Hersey, 1996, pp. 44–45).

Leadership styles identified with the styles of exercising power were pointed out by Kwiatkowski in his work entitled *Typologie przywództwa* (*Typologies of leadership*). The author distinguished the following leadership styles: a) autocratic (the leader, who is the "face of the group", makes autonomous decisions without consulting the group and is the main executor of the idea that unites the team); b) democratic (the leader makes decisions that are the result of a compromise obtained through discussions with group members and coordinates different options of action); c) permissive/liberal (the leader leaves the subordinates a lot of freedom in decision-making and takes on the role of advisor and expert themselves (Kwiatkowski, 2011, p. 14, after: Michalak, 2014, pp. 10–11).

Emphasising once again the fact that the first approaches to the issue of leadership took into account the necessity of choosing and applying an established leadership style, it is worth emphasising explicitly that contemporary approaches to the issue of leadership styles reveal a far-reaching flexibility in the selection of styles depending on the situational context. The more effective a leader is, the broader the repertoire of leadership styles he or she possesses and is able to adapt them to situational and environmental conditions. The evolutionary model of leadership developed by Hersey and Blanchard, referring to situational views of leadership, attaches particular importance to the category of the degree of "readiness" of employees and makes the adoption of the leadership style dependent on this. The prerequisite for effectiveness is a good knowledge of the employees and a focus on goals. Readiness is defined by the authors as a desire for achievement, a willingness to take responsibility and task-related talents, skills and experience (Stoner, Freeman & Gilbert, 2001, p. 463). A cognitively interesting reflection on the issue in question is presented by Blanchard and Hersey as they mention: when we published our article in 1969, the management hierarchy was functioning well and when the term situational leadership appeared, one could see the excitement in some managers and coaches, but it was still believed that it was the leaders and managers who had the power. The authors clearly conclude that, in fact, it was rare to include followers (*successors*) in discussions about their own development and career. The conceptual apparatus and terminology in place (supervisor, subordinate, manager, manual worker) reflected the quality of thinking and made the discussion on the concept difficult in the face of the existing cultural code. The authors, referring to the present day, emphasise the paradigm shift. They talk about leadership emphasising that it entails a change as it is an ongoing process, and they stress that leadership is created with people, not by people. To cope with the change, diversity and skills are needed in the following dimensions (styles): a) speaking and leading, b) persuasion and coaching, c) participation and support, d) delegation. In modern organisations, using situational leadership means emphasising task effectiveness and activity for change and improvement. When making decisions concerning tasks, it is important to effectively assess the needs of one's employee and divide tasks into subtasks. The authors emphasise that situational leadership is not about leadership *per se*, but about meeting the needs of employees (followers), as focusing on followers can improve leadership skills much more than teaching a specific leadership style (Blanchard & Hersey, 1996, pp. 44–45).

From the above, it can be concluded, as Hersey and Blanchard put it, that leadership style is not a fixed personality trait of a leader but a situational variable. As a result of empirical studies, researchers rejected the idea that there is a single ideal or universal leadership style and proved that, depending on the situational context, a team can (or rather should) be led by using different styles. Not irrelevant to the proposed thesis is the consideration of the degree of maturity of the functioning team members. It is the distinguished variable that mainly determines the choice of leadership style in order to motivate team members (it is important to know them well) to act in the most effective and efficient way (it is essential to define the organisation's objectives). Taking a high or low level of people orientation vs. task orientation as a benchmark, the researchers distinguished four leadership styles: a) selling/persuasion ("the degree of maturity of subordinates is rather high. The leader directs their actions, showing more confidence in the subordinates' competence. He or she tries to maintain a relationship with them, show support, convince them of his or her ideas, but makes most of the decisions themselves. The leader's role is to reduce task-oriented behaviour and increase relationship orientation to help the group build competence") (Michalak, 2014, pp. 12–13), (b) participation ("the degree of maturity of the subordinates is high enough to increase their scope of freedom and autonomy. The leader makes decisions together with the subordinates, focuses on the relationship with them and abandons determining the way how they should perform a task. He or she reduces the degree of involvement in the control of the task and in the relationship, so that the group can increase self-confidence and autonomy at work") (Michalak, 2014, pp. 12–13), c) delegation ("subordinates show a very high degree of maturity and commitment to their work, so the leader lets them go their own way, delegates tasks to the group and expects them to be accomplished. The art of leadership here is very much about knowing when to let people work on their own and assume the role of a supportive colleague. Clear delegation of tasks must be accompanied by demarcation of authority") (Michalak, 2014, pp. 12–13), d) commanding/directives ("the degree of maturity of subordinates is quite low. The leader displays behaviours that are highly task-oriented and far less relationship-oriented in order to help the group succeed and start learning. The leader defines the roles of subordinates, teaches them the right way to perform tasks") (Michalak, 2014, pp. 12–13).

Noteworthy are the situational variables, defined by Fiedler as "leadership situations", on which the choice of an effective leadership style depends. The author's empirical findings indicate that the quality of the leader-employee relationship has the greatest influence on the authority and effectiveness of leadership. The second most important variable in a leadership situation is task structure and the third is the position of authority. The combination of the highlighted variables in a leadership situation can determine eight possible leadership styles (Stoner, Freeman & Gilbert, 2001, pp. 466–467).

The distinguished diverse approaches to leadership styles integrate and synthesise a way of thinking, whose structural content points to many different cognitive perspectives, thus providing an overview of the undertaken studies and discourses. In the views of many authors, the discourse of power is directly or indirectly addressed. The co-existing theories, clearly indicate how leadership issues focus on the concept of power.

Power is understood as the source of leader's influence. Five potential sources of power can be distinguished:

(a) positional authority (the leader should clearly demonstrate his or her positional authority and it involves a sound working knowledge of the applicable law, existing economic opportunities, etc.). The distinguished body of knowledge gives the leader the parameters by which he or she can give directions and control the quality of his or her employees' work);

(b) the power of reward (leaders also use rewards – both financial and non-financial – to shape staff attitudes and behaviour. Kouzes and Posner, conducting research for a book entitled *Encouraging the Heart*, elicited the feedback from respondents that the most important non-financial reward employees can receive is simply a word: *thank you*. However, the research also showed that rewards are most effective when they are given for behaviours that leaders would like to see regularly in their employees; they are meaningful to the person you are thanking because they are related to what

is important to them; they are given randomly rather than in equal stretches of time; the nature and scale of rewards vary for different behaviours);
(c) coercive power (the use of coercive power, i.e. the imposition of consequences after the undesirable and unacceptable behaviour, has been shown to be effective in reducing such behaviour. However, while this method is in the leader's repertoire, it is advisable to use it with caution and good judgement, as it has also been proven to have a strong negative impact on the subsequent relationship);
(d) expertise (expertise is also a source of power because people are more likely to listen to the words of a leader when they believe the leader knows what they are talking about and, thus, lead others with a significant amount of expertise. When leaders guide people who have better functional expertise than they do, they can continue to improve their level of expertise by: staying up to date and sharing strategic initiatives with others, taking advantage of relevant development opportunities in the organisation where they work, reading professional industry press, gradually building their image as a competent leader);
(e) interpersonal power (interpersonal power, as research shows, is the most effective way of exerting influence in an organisation and means the ability to influence the behaviour of others simply because of the relationship they have with the leader. It is not insignificant that the younger generation feel more loyalty to a relationship than to an organisation, so the significance of this element further increases (Kilian, 2007, pp. 2–3)[3].

The literature also emphasises the importance of the bases of managerial power. The effectiveness of leadership may depend on the following sources of power: rewarding, enforcing power, appointment by law, reference or expertise. Both the ability to use and exercise various forms of power are important in expanding the possibilities for effective and efficient leadership (Stoner, Freeman & Gilbert, 2001, p. 453).

---

3 The author gives a telling example of the last component of power, namely: a word of 'thank you' from the mouth of someone who counts, whom we respect, is more important than a word 'thank you' from the mouth of someone who does not count. Similarly, the expression of disappointment is stronger when it comes from someone we respect, someone we care about.

Małgorzata Rosalska

Chapter II:
Leadership in school communities

The aim of this section of the book is to present how the concept of leadership discussed in Chapter I is perceived in education and what opportunities exist for implementing it into everyday educational practice. In determining the extent to which a school principal can perform the functions of a manager and leader, it is useful to refer to the key concepts of education and educational leadership, and to consider what factors shape thinking about the principal's role in the school community. To accomplish this, the key differences between leadership in education and educational leadership will be presented, as well as the roles and responsibilities of a school principal as a leader of those who constitute the school community.

2.1 Leadership in education

Analysing school as an organisation means focusing on the elements that constitute it. It can be described through its elements, the stakeholders, the ways in which services are provided, the structure for ordering the activities of its members, the organisational culture, external actors or events (De Toni & De Marchi, 2023, p. 74). One fundamental aspect is how processes and people are managed. In this context, school is a space where the way it is managed plays a considerable role in the design and implementation of everyday practices related to teaching, upbringing and care.

Leadership analysed in the context of educational processes can be seen both as a process and as characteristics of those who perform the tasks of managing and directing activities in the organisation. This includes such activities as conceptualising the school work, motivating performance and collaboration, and team building. Leadership as a characteristic is defined as a set of personality traits attributed to those who are perceived as leaders. Tony Bush defines leadership in education by identifying three dimensions that constitute it. In his view, it is a process of influence, which is linked to values and based on vision (Bush,

2011, pp. 5–7). Influence means that leadership always occurs in a social relationship and can involve both actions and relationships. Influence defined in this way is characterised by three features. Firstly, the author assumes that leadership is not dependent on the function held and is also independent of formal authority. This is, in his view, one of the characteristics that help distinguish leadership from management. The second characteristic is intentionality. The actions taken by a leader should always be directed towards the realisation of predetermined goals. The third characteristic of influence identified by Bush is that it can be developed by both individuals and groups (Bush, 2011, pp. 5–7).

According to the cited author, leadership in education is strongly linked to values. Bush even points out that leaders are expected to base their actions on clearly defined axiological assumptions (Bush, 2011, p. 6). These values can be analysed on two levels. The first concerns the intelligibility of individual values preferred, declared and taken into account in the actions performed by a leader. Those who are to some extent influenced by the leader have the right to know on what axiological grounds they take action and interpret the facts. In the context of the school principal's work, this is a very important issue, especially as axiological threads can be the basis for conflicts concerning the interpretation of educational objectives or preferred educational content. The second level of analysing axiological assumptions are the values which lay basis for the vision of school activity and the objectives derived from it. These values can be identified by analysing the curricular content, but also the artefacts of school daily life, the type of holidays and their celebration, the selection of collaborators from the social environment. The third feature of leadership implemented in the field of education is vision. However, as the author points out, the importance of vision in the leadership process is not obvious (Bush, 2011, p. 6). He observes that in the context of education, vision of a school principal as a leader can be challenging. The notion and concept of vision as an element of leadership originates from the business community, where the greatest innovators and successful people were referred to as visionaries in their industry or field. However, the school is not an individual principal's project. It is true that he or she are required to present their own ideas for the operation and development of the organisation they run, but this must be a vision that is consistent with the values and goals promoted throughout the education system.

The category of leadership is a concept that is not only of cognitive interest, but also intensely shapes the management of schools and influences approaches to the education of principals perceived as leaders of school communities. Hence, the need to analyse basic typologies of leadership in education seems justified. The content presented below demonstrates the diverse directions in which both leadership theory and also its practical applications have been developing.

Adopting this perspective of leadership analysis makes it possible, in a relatively orderly manner, to present different theoretical approaches.

The division between transactional and transformational leadership is widely known and analysed in educational contexts. It can be assumed that this is one of the basic perspectives for describing and analysing leadership in education. As these concepts have already been discussed in Chapter I, this part of the work will present the typology of leadership in education proposed by Tony Bush. It is an ordering account of the dominant contemporary fundamental approaches to educational leadership. The author identified ten models of leadership:
- managerial
- instructional
- transformational
- participative
- distributed
- transactional
- post-modern
- emotional
- contingent
- moral (Bush, 2011, pp. 201–204).

Managerial leadership is analogous to formal management models. It is often challenged and dismissed as limited and technical, however, it is an essential element of successful leadership, ensuring that the school's vision and strategy are pursued. This model starts from the premise that the overall indications set out in the vision and mission statements and the agreed objectives must be transformed into strategic and operational management. The implementation stage of the decision-making process is just as important as the development of the school vision. Management without vision is rightly criticised as managerialism; albeit, a vision without effective implementation always leads to frustration (Bush, 2011, p. 201).

Instructional leadership differs from other models in that it is more focused on direction than on the leadership process itself. It primarily emphasises the goals of education and stresses the need to focus on teaching and learning as the main tasks of educational institutions. In the view of T. Bush, however, this model has two main weaknesses. Firstly, it underestimates other important goals of education, including student well-being and the tasks connected with socialisation and developmental dynamics. It also marginalises the less academic aspects of education, including sport, theatre and music. The second objection relates to the focus on goals, without in-depth reflection on how to achieve them. In this respect it is, in the author's view, a limited and partial model (Bush, 2011, p. 201).

Transformational leadership is currently one of the most fashionable approaches to leadership in education, mainly because it corresponds to the dominant narratives describing contemporary leadership arrangements. The most important expectation directed at transformational leaders is related to taking actions that foster and enhance the level of engagement of all participants in the school community. This engagement is built through activities such as creating a vision, setting common goals or breaking down hierarchies, among others. Bush also draws attention to the limitations of this model. He indicates the risk of manipulation that teachers may be subjected to in order to implement the assumptions and values promoted by the leader (Bush, 2011, p. 201).

Participative leadership involves teachers and other stakeholder groups in the decision-making process. It is based on a broken hierarchy, cooperation and shared responsibility. This model emphasises collective decision-making, the distribution of responsibility for decision-making to specific individuals and groups, discussion and mediation. This approach is assumed to be effective in increasing participants' involvement and developing teamwork. However, it also has its limitations. Adherence to the principles of participation and collegiality can result in longer time needed to reach an agreement and a clearly defined role for the formal leader, who on the one hand is responsible for creating the conditions for debate and discussion, but on the other hand, still bears individual responsibility for decisions taken collectively (Bush, 2011, p. 202).

Distributed leadership has become the normatively preferred leadership model in the 21st century, replacing the participative model. It is distinguished from many other models by a stronger emphasis on collective decision-making. Tony Bush, referring to Kenneth Leithwood's research on the impact of school leadership, emphasises that leadership has a greater impact on schools and students if it is significantly distributed (Bush, 2011, p. 202).

In transactional leadership, the relationship between principals, teachers and other stakeholders relies on a process of exchange. Relationships between the two are based on conflicts of interest. Leaders offer rewards or incentives to their supporters, but do not seek to improve their commitment or intrinsic motivation, as the transformational model assumes. In its basic form, this model is revealed in employment contracts, in which the terms and conditions of employment are enumerated and the reward structure and processes made explicit. During day-to-day management, school principals can offer incentives such as promotions or raises, thereby convincing others to support their plans or take on certain tasks. The main limitation of the transactional model is that exchanges are usually short-lived and limited to the specific issue under discussion. It has little impact on teacher's behaviour or school performance. Transactional leadership does not result in long-term commitment to the values and visions promoted by school leaders (Bush, 2011, p. 203).

Postmodern leadership is very close to the subjective management model. It emphasises the need to consider multiple individual conditions. Reality is not seen here as objectively defined. Each participant in the life of school is given the right to unique, subjective assessments and interpretations of situations and processes. Instead of a single vision, formulated by leaders, there are multiple visions and diverse cultural meanings. The main limitation of this model, as with the similar subjective perspective, is that it offers little guidance for leadership action. It contributes to leadership theory mainly by focusing on individual insights and by emphasising the need to deal with people as individuals rather than as an undifferentiated group (Bush, 2011, p. 203).

Emotional leadership model emphasises the importance of individual motivation and interpretation of events. It is based on the assumption that emotions are socially constructed and are, at the same time, an indicator of meaning that an individual attributes to events, processes and phenomena. The way they are perceived, semanticized or interpreted is treated as reality. This model also assumes that it is emotions, not facts that shape attitudes and behaviour. Consequently, a rational approach is not sufficient to explain how leaders perceive and perform their role (Bush, 2011, p. 204).

Contingent leadership recognises the diverse nature of school context and the benefits of adapting leadership styles to specific situations, rather than adopting a single attitude that would be appropriate in all cases. Educational contexts are too complex and unpredictable to apply one leadership approach to all events and issues. Given the volatile, ambiguous environment, leaders must be able to identify the situation and adopt the most appropriate response to it. Thus, contingent leadership is not a single model, but represents an attitude of flexible response, which requires effective assessment and then prudent selection of the most appropriate leadership style. This model is pragmatic, but critics recognise its limitations due to its lack of grounding in principles. They also note that with this approach, it is difficult to take into account the holistic picture of the processes carried out in school (Bush, 2011, p. 204).

The moral leadership model is built on the leader's individual, subjectively defined values, beliefs and ethical assumptions. It is the leader who decides which resolutions and behaviours are evaluated as good or bad, as desirable or unacceptable. Ethical attitudes of the leader are the essential reference point here. This leadership model can be found in faith-based schools or in schools based on strongly defined axiologies. The fundamental problem here, however, is the conflict concerning the differences between the axiological, or spiritual, assumptions of the leader and other members of the school community (Bush, 2011, p. 204).

The typology discussed above reveals the dominant interpretive strands regarding leadership in education. However, this is not an exhaustive list. It is just one possible way of organising different perspectives of thinking about leadership in education. Another example is the division proposed by Yin-Cheong Chen, who analyses comprehensive leadership in education by looking at its six dimensions: technological leadership, economic leadership, social leadership, political leadership, cultural leadership and leadership in learning. The author emphasises that changes in different areas of life require a redefinition of the function of schools, but also a reflection on the possibilities for managing the development and effectiveness of schools in the context of such rapid civilizational transformations (Cheng, 2024, p. 70).

A similar position is taken by Michael Fullan, who notes that leadership in education has undergone a significant shift in recent years. This evolution is described by four phenomena: leadership is less linear, it requires leaders to continually learn and help others to learn, it requires greater precision and effectiveness in and through the group, and it makes local and broader contributions (Fullan, 2020). As a response to the changing context of education and the dynamic changes in the environment of schools, the author proposed the concept of educational leadership, which he called Nuance. It is an ability or set of habits that enable a leader to manage in context. This way of leadership is based on 4 elements, such as: experts in context, joint determination, culture of accountability and becoming a system player (Fullan, 2020).

Analysing the authors' proposed directions of change in the perception of leadership in education, one can see a shift towards participatory management and towards a greater use of resources and involving the potential of all the stakeholders forming school communities. It can be assumed that leadership in education will continue to evolve. This is conditioned by changes not only in school, but also in its social and cultural environment. Tony Bush, reflecting on the determinants of implementing leadership models in schools, identified five overlapping factors: the size of the institution, its organisational structure, the time allocated to management, the resources available and the external environment (Bush, 2011, p. 205). These are variables that significantly and dynamically model the way of thinking and acting in the field of educational leadership. One can get the impression that the characteristics of the organisation and its environment are nowadays more important in the processes of implementing theoretical concepts of leadership into educational practice than the individual characteristics and preferences of the school principal. It can therefore be assumed that new concepts and new proposals will constantly appear. The direction of these changes is to enhance the participation of all members of school life and its social environment and to build a culture that fosters cooperation. The level of acceptance of theoretical concepts and proposals for ways of working in school daily life will be conditioned both by the organisational culture of schools, the processes in the closer and further environment of a school, as well as the individual capacities, resources and beliefs of principals.

2.2 Educational leadership

Both in reflection on leadership and in everyday educational practices, it is important to emphasise differences in the perception of leadership in education and educational leadership. The most common terms found in literature to describe educational leadership are school leadership, educational leadership, managerial leadership and instructional leadership. The first concept worth explaining is school leadership. It is used to describe the overall management and organisational strategies of school processes. It should be emphasised that the term also means the management or organisation and governance of educational processes. The importance of school leadership is demonstrated by numerous empirical studies. It is worth referring here, for example, to the analyses carried out by Philip Hallinger and Ronald H. Heck, who showed a correlation between the principal's mode of leadership and the educational achievements among students (see: Hallinger & Heck, 1996, pp. 5–44). The authors analysed the available research on the impact of school leadership on student learning outcomes. They found that this influence can be described as indirect and is mainly due to such factors as the organisation of the school's social environment, forms of motivation for learning and support for learning (see: Hallinger & Heck, 1996, pp. 5–44).

Two research-based premises are particularly relevant in the area of school leadership, as Stephen L. Jacobson notes. The first is that, assuming all other factors are of equal value, schools with good leadership should outperform other schools. The second emphasises that school leadership is particularly important in schools located in communities at risk of marginalisation, with a significant proportion of pupils at risk of school failure (Jacobson, 2005, p. 457). Therefore, it can be assumed that the quality of school leadership plays a greater role in the more unfavourable the socio-economic environment in which a school operates. Analysing the research on school leadership, Alma Harris and Michell Jones pointed to five important findings from their analysis. They confirm the importance of effective school leadership not only in the context of school management, but also in the context of achieving teaching and learning goals:
- Effective School Leadership has a positive and lasting impact on organizational performance.
- Effective school leadership has a positive impact on learning and learner outcomes.
- Effective school Leadership is distributed widely and wisely.

- Effective School Leaders build collaborative practices and foster enquiry.
- Effective School Leaders are System Leaders (Harris & Jones, 2023, pp. 449-453).

An illustration of thinking in terms of school leadership is also the model proposed in the publication *The Making of Leadership in Education. A European Qualification Network for Effective School Leadership.* This work is interesting because it is based on the analysis of European researchers and educational practitioners. The authors developed a model built around five basic domains, each of which contains detailed components. These are as follows: the political and cultural demands on school and their translation into the internal sense and direction of schools; understanding and empowering teachers and other staff; building structure and appropriate cultural role models; cooperation with partners and the external environment; and personal development of leaders (Framework of Reference, 2011). This extended and detailed model of school leadership provides an opportunity to recognise how many areas affect the quality and effectiveness of a school. It is a model that situates school in a broader – social, cultural, but also economic – context. It is, therefore, possible to conclude that leadership understood in this way allows the principles of school's work to be aligned with its wider environment.

Another concept that is relevant to the undertaken analysis is educational leadership, which is extremely difficult to interpret. It is hard to find full, clear and conclusive definitions of this concept in the literature. Grzegorz Mazurkiewicz defines it as "a process that concerns teaching and learning processes" (Mazurkiewicz, 2011, p. 26). While school leadership can be assumed to encompass the leadership of all processes carried out in a school, educational leadership is a subset of these processes and encompasses those that relate to the teaching and learning process. Its aim is to "create the conditions for individual and organisational learning" (Mazurkiewicz, 2011, p. 26). Thus, it can be assumed that school leadership comprises two particularised areas – managerial leadership, covering the organisational aspect of school work, and educational leadership, aimed at the effective implementation of basic school functions, i.e. building an environment conducive to learning. It is important to note that the term educational leadership can be used both to "denote leadership relating to the educational sphere and leadership conducive to the shaping appropriate educational conditions for the development of all subjects involved in education" (Michalak, 2010, p. 190). This means it can be used to analyse and describe processes not only in school, but also in its social environment.

A special significance in the field of educational leadership should be attributed to what is referred to as instructional leadership. Although it is sometimes seen as just one type of educational leadership, it is worth focusing on. It is particularly interesting because much of the research on the relationship between educational leadership and student achievement is based on the instructional leadership model. Researchers identify the relationship and co-dependence between individual behaviour of the principal and the educational outcomes of students.

Philip Hallinger, who has analysed the development of the concept of instructional leadership, observes that it has clearly evolved not only in terms of theoretical assumptions, but also as an educational practice. The author argues that research conducted in the 1980s on the determinants of school effectiveness focused the attention of educational policy makers and researchers on the potential of those responsible for the functioning of individual schools for many years. Despite some criticism, this was the dominant perspective on school leadership for many years. It was not until the 1990s that alternative narratives emerged, among them the distinctive concept of transformational leadership. Hallinger notes that while it may have seemed that instructional leadership would lose its prominence, the concept has once again gained name and popularity in the context of new educational challenges. In the author's view, general trends in education – globalisation and a clear focus on performance of both individual students and schools – have contributed to this. However, this return to the idea of leadership, particularly instructional leadership, is no longer simply a recreation and evocation of assumptions developed in the 1980s. It is nowadays referred to as leadership for learning (Hallinger, 2010, p. 61).

Various models of instructional leadership can be found in the literature, but the most popular is the one developed by Philip Hallinger and Joseph Murphy (Hallinger & Murphy, 1985, pp. 217–248). The authors identified three of its key dimensions: defining the school's mission, managing the curriculum and creating positive school atmosphere. These three important tasks are made more specific by referring to specific responsibilities of the leader. The first dimension is defining the mission of school. The word purpose is also used instead of the word mission (Hallinger & Murphy, 1985, p. 221). In this approach, the purposes are not concerned with the general objectives of school work, but are oriented towards their didactic aspect. The authors identified two specific tasks here: formulating clear, comprehensible and understandable purposes of the school work and communicating them effectively. This dimension focuses the principal on the most important tasks, gives perspective and purpose. In practice, this means constantly making sure that the school has clear, measurable and time-dependent objectives aimed at the progress of pupils in terms of learning outcomes. It is the principal's responsibility to communicate these purposes in such a way that they are not only widely known, but also motivate the whole school community to facilitate the process of achieving them (Hallinger, 2010, p. 66). The authors also emphasise that the purposes so understood should not be equated with learning outcomes. Objectives, in contrast to the assumptions about outcomes described in the core curriculum, are defined by the school principal in cooperation with other staff members. It is essential that they are developed in such a way that they can be implemented in everyday educational practice. This, in turn, requires special care to ensure that they are known, accepted and understood not only by teachers, but also by pupils and their parents (Hallinger & Murphy, 1985, p. 222).

The second dimension of the instructional leadership model is the management of the curriculum implementation process. This includes attention to the quality of methodology as well as legal and organisational aspects of curriculum implementation. Hallinger and Murphy identified three specific tasks: supervision and evaluation of day-to-day educational practices of specific teachers in the classroom, coordination of curriculum implementation and monitoring of students' progress. The principal is required to be involved in strengthening learning and teaching processes, with simultaneous supervision and monitoring. These issues require that he or she should have the competence and experience to carry out teaching tasks and to engage in the strengthening of school. This means that a principal in this model should be characterised by methodological competence and pedagogical preparation. This dimension of leadership relates primarily to working with teachers. Hallinger notes here a danger of placing too much emphasis on the aspect of supervision and control. He points out that the task of a principal is mainly to create opportunities and ensure the professional development of teachers, especially in the effective use of methodological solutions that facilitate achieving the objectives defined in the mission of the school (Hallinger, 2010, p. 67).

The third dimension describes the tasks involved in creating atmosphere conducive to learning. This dimension is broader in scope than the previous two. The authors distinguished here such tasks as: managing the time allocated to teaching, supporting teachers' professional development, maintaining a high degree of transparency in the undertaken activities, building teachers' and students' motivation, and developing high requirements and standards (Hallinger, 2010, p. 67). This area of activity concerns norms and attitudes of both students and employees. The authors start with the premise that it is the principal who creates the favourable framework for achieving the stated purposes. By clearly formulating expectations and standards and by creating conditions for work and designing a system of reinforcement, the principal influences individual attitudes and behaviour, both among pupils and among teachers.

Today, this model is evolving towards the concept of leadership for learning. Increasing importance is given to organisational and methodological solutions that can positively or disruptively model the learning process. As P. Hallinger notes, contemporary research on educational leadership, points to the need to search for specific, educational factors that enable the construction of environment conducive to learning. The authors attribute more importance in this regard to the competences associated with instructional leadership than to the theoretical assumptions of transformational leadership (Hallinger, 2010, p. 69).

2.3 Principal as a leader

The literature offers many suggestions for competency profiles of a principal as a leader of school community. These tend to emphasise two elements: the characteristics of a leader and the competencies needed to perform leadership tasks. Reflections on the differences in the desirable characteristics of a leader and a manager are presented in Chapter 3.2. In this part of the work, three selected reflections on the description of a leader's role in an educational context will be discussed.

The first of the proposed perspectives on the analysis of school principal's role as a leader refers to their core functions. The direction of interpretation of leader's role in the school community will be determined by the definition proposed by Błażej Smykowski. According to this author, "a leader is a person who effectively leads people in the process aimed at realising their own needs" (Smykowski, 1996, p. 57). In terms of the role thus described, the leader undertakes four basic leadership functions:
- animation of initiatives,
- mediating needs,
- counselling,
- care (Smykowski, 1996, p. 64).

In the scope of initiative animation, the following activities are indicated: recognising the needs of all groups that constitute the school community and those that aspire to shape the direction and purpose of the school, organising and coordinating the work of individual groups and teams, motivating people to act together. Mediation of needs, on the other hand, is aimed at mediating between the interests of individuals and groups, pointing to available solutions, to the context, rules, law, and available resources. The role of school principal as a mediator is particularly important. It can even be assumed that one of the key roles of the principal as a leader is to reconcile the interests of individuals with those of school as a community. Also, there are tasks related to the development of conflict-management skills in all partners. Providing information about legal, administrative and economic frameworks that set the boundaries of possible mediation is an important educational aspect that prepares all stakeholders for substantive discussions and constructive search for common ground. The third leadership function, the advisory one, involves activities focused on the specialised aspect of the performed tasks. In school context, this means that the principal is expected to strive for professional development within the scope of the activities entrusted to them, and at the same time to undertake activities, e. g. education and counselling, which enable pupils, teachers and parents to obtain specialised, factually sound and up-to-date information regarding the processes and phenomena of interest. The last function is of a caring nature. The leader's task in this respect is to defuse negative tensions and emotions, to build a good atmosphere that is conducive to team work, and to seek compromises and resources for conflict resolution (Smykowski, 1996, pp. 64–65).

This division of leadership functions not only helps outline the tasks to be performed by a school principal. It is also a useful format for evaluating the competence of principals in the four functions indicated and, consequently, the basis for developing projects aimed at working in the area of diagnosed deficits. This simple division of functions stems from the author's perception of the role of a leader as someone who is supposed to help fulfil the needs of those with and for whom they work.

Another perspective on leadership focuses on the concept of attitude. This approach has been proposed by Jacek Pyżalski, who, starting from the three-component concept of attitude, highlighted the possibility of recognising the leadership potential of principals in three dimensions: knowledge, attitudes and behaviours (Pyżalski, 2014, p. 15). Intrestingly this model emphasises the importance of the emotional-evaluative component, which includes judgements, opinions, beliefs and attitudes. These are strongly dynamic factors in the actions revealed by the behavioural component of attitude. What actions a principal takes and what actions he or she abandons or limits may be the result of adopted judgements, opinions, and attitudes. It is worth noting that this aspect is often overlooked in proposals for principal-leader competence profiles. Much more weight is attached to individual qualities and competences defined by a set of knowledge and skills. As noted above, most of the proposals for analysing the competency profile of a school principal are postulatory. They are mostly proposals for theoretical models that can be used to assess the resources of a principal or can be a rationale for developing offers addressed to principals or to candidates for this position. Therefore, I consider as particularly interesting the data illustrating how principals actualise their individual concepts of realising themselves as principals.

The third perspective for analysing the role of a school principal as a leader, we wish to offer, consists of various types of standards developed by bodies concerned with the quality of leadership in education and with supporting the development of management in education. For the purposes of this publication, we will invoke the standards developed by the *National Policy Board for Edu-*

cational Administration. The proposed standards define the nature and quality of the work of educational leaders. They specify how to prepare for the professional role, indicate directions for development and criteria for assessment and evaluation of the work. The authors of this document have identified 10 standards which are as follows:
1. Mission, Vision, and Core Values
2. Ethics and Professional Norms
3. Equity and Cultural Responsiveness
4. Curriculum, Instruction, and Assessment
5. Community of Care and Support for Students
6. Professional Capacity of School Personnel
7. Professional Community for Teachers and Staff
8. Meaningful Engagement of Families and Community
9. Operations and Management
10. School Improvement (Professional Standards for Educational Leaders, 2015).

In the aforementioned document, these general standards are made more specific and operationalised. They provide precise guidance not only as to what qualities and skills should characterise a leader in education, but also set directions for their professional development.

The advantage of standards developed by various bodies is that they are concerned with quality and professionalism of the undertaken activities. However, these are demands and guidelines for building individual professionalism. They can provide a cue for local politicians or institutions overseeing the quality of education in particular local authorities. They can also provide a matrix for evaluating ideas for the role of school principal presented during recruitment for the position. The third advantage of standards is their potential in designing development programmes for school leaders.

A fundamental issue, which is not resolved by standards although they indicate its importance, is the problem of diagnosing the actual and not just the declarative competencies and qualities of school leadership candidates or assessing the resources of those carrying out leadership roles. This is an issue that is well recognised in business situations, where methods such as 360-degree Feedback or Assessment/Development Centre are a widely accepted and used strategy for assessing employee's resources, especially when they are in a leadership or managerial role. In terms of assessing leadership competence, it should be carefully considered who is given the authority to assess the competence of school leaders. In the context of the increasingly promoted ideas of participative governance, this question is gaining significance.

Agnieszka Cybal-Michalska

Chapter III:
"Management" – selected theoretical approaches

3.1 Management – the evolution of the notion and variety of definitions

Both the practice and theoretical foundations of management date back to the 19th century. Management, on the other hand, as an academic discipline, can be traced back to the second half of the 20th century. It is believed that the greatest contribution to the development of the discourse on management was made by Drucker (Darr, 2011, p. 7).

In considering the definitional *credo* of the term "management", one starts from the Latin phrase *manuagere*, which means to lead someone by holding their hand. In this sense, leading by hand means giving guidance. The term, as Shied notes, also suggests that the person leading goes first by themselves to where they then want to lead someone else. One property of management is undoubtedly its relational nature. According to Drucker, management simply means "doing things" with the help of other people. The teleological dimension of management is not insignificant. According to Weijrich and Koontz, management is the process of planning, leading, organizing and controlling people in a group to achieve goals, but also creating an action plan (strategy) and controlling the required strategic and operational activities to achieve effective management (Mahmood, Muhammad & Bashir, 2012, p. 513). Bohoris and Vorria speak in a similar vein. The authors provide a framework for conceptualizing the issue of management by referring to the metaphorical sense. Referring to attempts to liken management to an art or a science, as well as referring to calling management an art or a science, they suspend the argument. They claim that it is not what management is compared to that is most important, but that its essence is the processual nature that serves to achieve organizational goals. Thus, it is a process that enables the organization to accomplish, what the organization needs to accomplish (Bohoris & Vorria, 2007, p. 2).

The above strand of considerations is reflected in the definitional findings of Bennis and Nanus. The authors define management as the execution of tasks and mastery of procedures. Rost, on the other hand, argues that management is one-way leadership, and Zaleznik believes that management requires different type of people than leadership (Ricketts, 2009, p. 2).

Middle and high-level managers spend most of their time solving problems. The circumstances surrounding problem solving tend to be complex, (not infrequently go beyond structure and routine) and require a lot of work. Problem solving consists of the following steps: a) identifying the problem including collecting and evaluating information), b) making logical assumptions c) developing preliminary alternatives and selecting those on which to focus more attention, d) evaluating alternatives by applying decision-making criteria, e) selecting the alternative that best fits the established criteria, f) implementing the solution, g) evaluating the results of the implementation (Darr, 2011, p. 12).

The lack of unified thought on the topic of capturing leadership and management makes it necessary to seek resolutions that show the universals and specific elements of both constructs. A separate subsection is devoted to this topic later in the paper. However, already at this point it is worth emphasizing that the two terms are semantically different. And although, after all, a subject can exercise management duties as well as leadership, managing will be identified with the performance of managerial, administrative and supervisory duties so as to give direction to a group or organization. But on the other hand, the framework of both conceptual constructs takes into account influencing others, related to working with other people and achieving a goal. Suffice it to say, therefore, that although the distinguished domains are semantically different, they need not exist completely separately, for when managers engage in influencing a group of employees to achieve intended goals, one can then already speak of leadership. Conversely, when leaders engage in aspects such as planning, organizing, staffing, or controlling, their activities take on managerial characteristics (Ricketts, 2009, p. 2).

3.2 Management theories

The phenomenon of management development can be analytically and interpretively looked at from different theoretical perspectives with different conceptual assumptions. Attempts to classify them, although they have a well-established tradition, are difficult to clearly organize the multitude of approaches. The reasons for this fact should be sought in the very nature of the discourse referring to the most general level of cognition, involving the adoption of a specific theory that determines the quality of cognition, description, diagnosis, exploration and possibility of understanding the phenomenon.

Cognitive practice and expectations of the explanatory qualities of claims (their accuracy) formulated by a theory (while reflecting on its explanatory capacity in general) refer to the ability to theoretically generalize and classify the phenomenon of cognition, or to translate theoretical theses into empirical cognition for verification, as well as to explain phenomena by identifying underlying causal mechanisms and processes revealed through the quality of their effects (Scott & Marshall, 2009, p. 761). And while sociological theory "as a practice and as an instrument of cognition of social reality is subject to external criticism as to the extent to which it meets universal scientific criteria, and at the same time is subject to self-assessments that point to positive or potentially developmental aspects of its autonomous cognitive status" (Misztal, 2000, p. 173), its cognitive value consists in a form representing the structure of a selected social phenomenon, among which the domain of management can be classified.

In this sense, it seems important to define the boundaries of the cognitive field allowing to specify whether the theory captures "'whole', 'most', and 'most important part' (…) in the range of variation of determinants or components of *explanandum*" (Misztal, 2000, p. 181)[4], and thus the object of cognition (understood as "something" to be explained) which is to be clarified. The explanatory capacity of a theory, and management theories are not free from this feature, is determined by recognizing the magnitude of the scope of reality to which the theory is applicable, therefore, it is "derived from the interrogative practices coupled into the cognitive process and depends on (…) whether they take into account comparative, historical and theoretical factors" (Misztal, 2000, p. 183). The cognitive status of the theory, which would allow to understand the phenomenon of management in the context of changes and permanent fluctuation of reality, is essential. This fact brings attention to the problem of "a theoretical character of many findings" (Manterys & Mucha, 2009, p. VII) and accumulation of social knowledge codified within the framework of distinguished paradigms. In the face of the dynamics of development and the hard-to-predict direction of social change, there may arise, as R. Baudon points out, a tendency "to conduct interim interrogative practices and to provide *ad hoc* answers to questions about the relationships between various elements of social reality. (…) 'A good theory … has an explanatory capacity that covers a range of

---

[4] The author emphasises that a theory can be satisfactory both when it encompasses "most" of the determinants of the *explanadum* and when it concentrates on "a smaller part of it", assuming, however, that it has at its disposal "such a significant recognition of the field of variability that allows one to conclude that the components which are the object of cognitive practice are in fact more heuristically significant" (ibidem, p. 182) than those omitted – less significant for the explanation of the chosen fragment of social reality.

relevant facts, including facts not yet known'" (after: Misztal, 2000, p. 189–190). Many theoretical orientations are subject to devaluation. When exposed to a critical examination that shows their limitations, they direct thinking toward "the need to develop new analytical instruments" (Manterys & Mucha, 2009, p. VII) relating to the quality of management in a dynamic process of change. In light of the above considerations, the constitutive feature of a "good" theory is its discursive character, "its openness to phenomena and processes not yet known, its acceptance of theoretical dialogue, and (...) its principled admission of the assumption regarding the historical variability of its own explanatory capacity" (Misztal, 2000, pp. 189–190). What constitutes the essence of modern "theorizing" is not limited to the debate around a general theory, but also to the applicability of the findings made in isolated sub-disciplines (Manterys & Mucha, 2009, pp. VIII–IX).

Refining the above discussion of the essence of sociological theorizing and its "fertility", the problem of understanding a "theory" arises. The extensive scientific debate devoted to this issue (which by no means aspires to be unambiguous in establishing the definitional credo of the term "theory") allows us to adopt the understanding of theory as "a deductive system, with a clearly defined set of assumptions and abstract basic statements of the highest degree of generality (preferably axioms) from which lower-order statements are derived" (Manterys & Mucha, 2009, p. XIII). Axioms, quite frequently not explicitly formulated in theories, are assumptions, postulates, universally received principles, or self-evident truths (Scott & Marshall, 2009, p. 33). The general definition of the term "theory", according to S. Nowak, emphasizes that it is "a set of laws (statements) ordered so that they can constitute a certain internally consistent logical structure." (Nowak, 1970, p. 370, after: Ziółkowski, 2006, p. 16). A theory explains and interprets phenomena, "trying to get to the possibly universal essence of the mechanisms that guide social processes and the sustenance and dynamics of structures" (Manterys & Mucha, 2009, p. XIII), which is further actualized by the need for a new view on social structure and social practices, to which management undoubtedly belongs. Even with Merton's postulate of building a middle-range theory (Marshall, 2005, p. 393), illustrating the desire to theorize selected aspects and manifestations of social life, theories "should be based on conceptual models of social reality, that is, certain general interrelated hypotheses about which of their features and what relationships between these features are considered particularly important" (Manterys & Mucha, 2009, p. XIII), which also creates the possibility of anticipating the direction and scope of social phenomena. The definition of the essence of a theory, proposed by J. Szacki, takes into account the awareness that a theory, which would meet all the conditions, simply does not exist. In the author's view, a theory "is any set of concepts and relatively general statements about social reality, intended to organize the available knowledge about it and provide guidelines for further observations and research" (after: Ziółkowski, 2006, p. 17).

Management theories can be included in Merton's classification of a middle-range theory. This prominent American sociologist, the author of work entitled *Social Theory and Social Structure*, defines middle-range theories as follows: "theories that fall between the not very momentous but necessary working hypotheses that arise in excess in the course of daily research work and constitute the most general consistent attempts to develop a unified theory with which one could explain the regularities evident in organizational behaviour and social change" (Marshall, 2005, p. 393). Hypotheses of momentous theoretical and cognitive importance include the recognition that management consists of four main elements. The attributes of "management" include the processual, structural and functional dimensions, namely: (1) it is a process, consisting of interconnected social and technical functions and activities (2) aimed at realizing the goals of the organization; (3) these goals are realized with the help of people and other means; (4) the process takes place in the formal environment of the organization (Darr, 2011, p. 8).

The main findings on management in selected theoretical orientations will be discussed below. Scientific management theory defines four principles of management aimed at increasing efficiency. Taylor's work was recognized by industrialists at the time. The principles he described, although they have an established history, are still being practiced. This is revealed, for example, by the fact that, the remuneration of employees depends on their efficiency. Modern management theorists, to mention Deming and Juran, also support Taylor's proposed principles and division of labour. And here they are:

1. "A science of work" should be developed. It means using a scientific method to study work and determining the best way to do it. It involves gathering information about different ways to perform a given task. Try different methods to find the best one.
2. A new method should be chosen and an employee should be selected and trained to perform the task in the best possible way. Employees should be selected according to the tasks assigned to them and provided with appropriate training according to their position in the organization to increase their efficiency.
3. Work training method should be selected to train some employees to get the best result. This means that those employees whose tasks fit the new rules should be chosen. Remuneration should be linked to productivity. Those who have achievements should be well motivated.
4. In order to perform various tasks efficiently and economically, these tasks and the responsibilities associated with them should be divided between employees and management (Mahmood, Muhammad & Bashir, 2012, p. 516).

While proving accurate in formulating and testing the theory of scientific management, the theory has received a great deal of criticism. The contestation initiative started at grassroots. Labour unions felt that the highlighted philosophy focused more on manual labour, for which the worker was paid less. In their view, it had a dehumanizing character. They condemned the pace of work and the inability of workers to voice their opinions and change the status quo. Man has stepped down in favour of the system and is treated like a machine. The theory was therefore considered to be directed against man (or even humanity), who had lost their position of being in the first place (Mahmood, Muhammad & Bashir, 2012, pp. 516–517).

Among the group of well-known classical management theories there is the administrative management theory developed by Fayol in 1916. Fayol proposed a theory based on his own experience, hence it is called Fayol's administrative theory in literal sense. It takes a theoretical-cognitive approach to business management and management in general. Fayol introduced six functions and fourteen principles of management. Among the functions of management, he lists: forecasting, planning, organizing, commanding, coordinating, and monitoring. In theorizing about management principles, he referred to the following variables: division of labour, power, discipline, quality of leadership, subordination of the interests of individuals to the interests of the whole, remuneration, centralization, scalar chain, order, equality, stability of personnel tenure, initiative, and sense of community. Referring to the *division of labour*, Fayol believed that specialisation in work was the best use of human resources, hence work had to be divided between individuals and groups in order to be efficient and certain that the effort and attention would be concentrated on specific spheres of the task. In the context of *power*, the theorist considered responsibility to be a term close to power. He defined authority as the right to give orders and having the power to enforce obedience, while responsibility means that one can rely on someone. In this sense, responsibility is part of power, for having power means also having responsibility. *Discipline and unity of leadership* play a key role in a successful organisation. Community thinking dictates that the interests of individuals *should be subordinated to the interests of the whole.* General interests and benefits should be given more priority. *Remuneration* of employees should not be based on a single variable such as productivity, but also on other variables, which include the cost of living, qualified staff, general business conditions and the success of a particular business. The author leans towards *centralisation.* However, according to Fayol, centralisation or decentralisation of management should be chosen depending on the needs or culture of the organisation. If for Fayol centralisation means reducing the importance of the role of subordinates, decentralisation means the opposite. The *scalar chain* is the necessity for a management hierarchy. Authority should be held by each manager, with top managers having the most authority and lower-level managers reporting to higher-level managers on their work. The existence of *order* in an organisation is an indication of the activities in the organization – their efficiency and effectiveness. *Equality* in an organisation is understood as embracing the principle that all employees should be treated as equally as possible, and this means that if the organisation is to succeed, the basic rights, rules and regulations should be the same for all employees, assuming that it should be clear that salaries cannot be distributed equally. Fayol believes that in a successful organisation, remuneration and other privileges should be awarded *according to seniority in the organisation*. Management should encourage employees' own initiative, as it is essential for the continuous improvement of the organisation. Today we can say that it is responsible for the quality of a learning organisation. Management should build a sense of community, harmony and well-being among employees (according to the saying "strength lies in unity") which increases productivity (Mahmood, Muhammad & Bashir, 2012, pp. 517–519).

The Bureaucratic Theory of Management developed in 1947 by a German sociologist Max Weber (Karl Emil Maximilian) or Weber's Theory of Bureaucracy based the structural idiom of management on principles referring to the existence of the following: written rules (standardised, defined and written rules and regulations), system-task relationships (establishment of a system for the performance of tasks and establishment of relationships between these structures), specialised trainings (problems in line with their assigned tasks), hierarchy of authority (pyramid of management, assignment of authority to managers according to their position in the company), clearly defined responsibilities (clear responsibilities and reporting procedure), formalisation (there should be a recording system in the organisation which corresponds directly to the activity in line with planning), a fair evaluation and reward system (the existence of an evaluation system rewarding employees who show commitment and competence), and a perfect bureaucracy (created by a system of trainings and rewards) (Mahmood, Muhammad & Bashir, 2012, pp. 519–520).

To summarise and, at the same time, elaborate on the problem addressed in this subchapter, it is worth referring to the two dominant theoretical perspectives ordering the reflections on the essence of management. Functionalist discourse dominates the way we think about organisations. Furthermore, the problem of management development is based on functionalist assumptions mainly directed towards the issue of performance in organisations ignoring many others, which are not addressed at all. The constructivist discourse does not look at the issue of management and management development as objective realities, but as something highly empirical and subjective. Managerial development is not just limited to programmes and structured activities, but can originate from and contribute to all kinds of social practices. However, the constructivist discourse is not free of explanatory problems because it is not equipped to explain the tensions between the needs of an individual and the needs of an organisation (e.g.: Mabey & Finch-Lees, 2008, pp. 78–100).

3.3 Management models and variations

A detailed interpretation of the theoretical assumptions regarding the essence of management shows that in order to understand what management is, it will be fundamental to refer to its models and variations. Without abandoning the discussion in this field, it is worth reflecting on the considerations of H. Mintzberg. The author, without omitting the important topic of management models, states that those who claim that management means controlling (as H. Fayol wanted) or acting (as T. Peters believed), or thinking and analysing (as M. Porter emphasised) are wrong. In the author's opinion, management cannot be reduced to the distinguished aspects, but comprises all of them. Management is not a collection but a system, it is not a sum but a combination of these roles. In the model of a holistic approach to management, the author distinguished three planes, assigning to each of them two roles that are important for the work of a manager. Thus, at the level of information, the important role is that of communication and control; at the interpersonal level, the role of directing (leadership) and establishing and maintaining contacts; and at the level of action, the role of organiser of current affairs and negotiator of the quality of transactions with stakeholders occupies a special place (Mintzberg, 2013, pp. 62–63, 68–69). It is worth emphasising that in the proposed model, a manager is at the centre, and the planes and roles are the arena in which the essence of management takes place.

It should also be remembered that a universal component of management is the dynamics of group processes. The quality aspect of group development was highlighted by Blanchard and Hersey. The authors distinguished four styles of management, while pointing to the relational nature of the process. The first style, the essence of which is management, emphasises its appropriateness for the orientation stage, in which objectives and roles must be precisely defined. The second style, coaching, is crucial for a constructive transition through the dissatisfaction phase, when a group needs to be guided, listened to, supported and encouraged. When the group reaches the resolution stage, the leader's style can take on a supportive character (style 3). The logic behind the fourth style is that an outside observer is unable to see who the leader is. This style is called delegating (Blanchard & Hersey, 1996, p. 45). An interesting aspect was highlighted by Bray. The results of longitudinal studies on management success indicate that it can be predicted, as it depends on the following characteristics: leadership and administration skills, high work motivation and orientation towards development and career, cognitive abilities, independence of thought and action, and task stability.

Małgorzata Rosalska

Chapter IV:
Empowerment as a strategy for management of educational processes

Empowerment is a concept related to management and exercising power, which is oriented towards delegating authority, leveraging employee resources and creating conditions for development. It is also a way of thinking about leading others, strategic management and systemic approach. It is a way of management that is particularly suited to managing organisations where people are the primary resource. Such organisations include schools and other educational and developmental institutions.

The perspective of process management in educational institutions is conditioned on many levels. Legal conditions are fundamental here, whether in the area of educational law, administrative law or labour law. However, many processes are also related to the leadership style, the way power is exercised and shared, the perception of the goals of managing people, processes and resources. The aim of this chapter is to show how and in which areas the foundations of empowerment can be used in the management of educational processes. The starting point is the assumption that empowerment can be an attractive concept for those school principals who not only embrace the ideas of the empowerment of the participants in the learning process, but also seek solutions to foster its implementation in everyday educational practices. Empowerment, understood as a way of management aimed at building a community of people jointly creating learning situations and supporting the learning process, stands in opposition to the traditionally understood hierarchy typical of conventional schools, where rules of authority are clearly established and consistently respected. This mode of management does not overturn established roles and relationships, rather it creates new contexts for collaboration, cooperation and shared responsibility. Rather than demolishing traditionally constructed hierarchies, it flattens their structure, allows horizontal relationships to be built, teaches undertaking initiative and the associated responsibilities.

In this chapter, the concept of empowerment will be discussed in selected aspects. In addition to providing a definition of the concept, its applied values for the management of educational processes will be pointed out. Empowerment will be discussed as a way of exercising power and as a perspective for diagnosing resources. These perspectives seem to be of particular relevance not only in terms of managing school processes, but above all in terms of taking real action related to building a school as a learning community.

4.1 Empowerment – definitions

The concept of empowerment originates from social work. It has a long tradition there, not only as a strategy for providing social support, but also as a way of thinking about the management of assistance processes. The concept was first proposed by Barbara B. Solomon in 1976 (see: Solomon, 1976; Herriger, 2002, p. 19). Since then, thinking in terms of empowerment, strengthening resources for co-participation and co-determination has also been adopted in other fields of work with people (Tengland, 2008, pp. 77–96). The concept is also used in management science. In the literature in this field, empowerment is referred to not only as a strategy, a philosophy, a management method, but also as a process or set of managerial practices (Moczydłowska, 2013, pp. 15–23). It is derived from motivation theory, social learning theory and the concepts of self-management, work design and participative management (Bugdol, 2006, p. 46).

The term empowerment functions in Polish in its original version, the word has no Polish equivalent[5]. The dictionary explains it as follows: empower sb. – to give someone self-confidence, to give someone control over their own life; empower sb. to do sth. – to give someone power of attorney, to authorize someone to do something; empowerment – authority, proxy (Fisiak, 2003).

Empowerment is defined in many ways. Depending on the discipline in which the definition is formulated, different dimensions of empowerment are emphasised. In social work, "it encompasses concepts between two extremes: teaching people to improve their socio-economic situation by struggling to change the system of social redistribution of wealth and teaching people to improve their situation through individual resourcefulness" (Szmagalski, 1994, pp. 121–122). It can also be understood as a process of empowering vulnerable, socially or economically inefficient, disadvantaged, marginalised people to take care of their own needs, or as a state of activation and resourcefulness. This view of empowerment is close to the concept of Barbara Solomon and her idea of restoring strength and agency to excluded and marginalised individuals and communities.

---

5 Similarly, in the literature on management and social work, the term is not translated in publications in German, French, Italian, Spanish.

In management science, empowerment is seen primarily as a technique, a way, a management process (Bugdol, 2006, p. 48). It can be defined both as "a human resource management technique that incorporates the transfer of power and control, from higher levels of the organizational structure to lower ones" (Bugdol, 2006, p. 48, after: Conger & Kanungo, 1988, pp. 471–482), "and as a process of building, developing and increasing the real impact of employees on the functioning of the organization through cooperation, division of tasks and responsibilities" (Bugdol, 2006, p. 48, after: Rothstein, 1995). Definitions that emphasise the processual character of this type of management are also proposed. In this view, empowerment can be understood following Ken Blanchard as "the process of unleashing the power latent in employees – their knowledge, experience and motivation – and directing this power to achieve results" (Blanchard, 2010, p. 58). According to Jane Smith, the management process so understood includes both motivation, management by commitment and management by delegation (Smith J., 2006, p. 8).

Marek Bugdol observes that in the field of management science, empowerment can be analysed in four basic dimensions: organisational, psychological, pedagogical and sociological. The organisational dimension is concerned with structure and describes its organisation and flexibility. The psychological component describes the level of integration of the organisation, its culture, skills and beliefs, determination and perception of impact. The pedagogical dimension is about development and skills, the formation of supervisor-subordinate relationships and staff training. The last component, i. e. sociological, describes power relations, the development of the organisational bond and normative integration (Bugdol, 2006, p. 50). These dimensions relate to general concepts of organisational management, but in the context of the subject of this book, the dimensions proposed by the author may be useful for the diagnosis and analysis of selected aspects of school understood as a learning organisation.

In Polish pedagogy, this concept is used more and more frequently. Although it is not present in the pedagogical dictionary as a term, there are more and more publications indicating both the theoretical aspects of this concept and examples of its use in pedagogical practice (see: Rosalska, 2006). In analysing the ways in which empowerment is invoked in pedagogical literature, Tony Lawson points out that empowerment can be understood as a general way of delegating decision-making capacity to "clients" in the educational relationship, i. e. as a shift of power from the level of the principal to the level of a teacher and from the level of a teacher to the level of a student, but also as a process in which participants in the school community develop competences that enable them to take responsibility for their own development and solve their own problems (Lawson, 2011). The author, citing the analyses conducted by Michalinos Zembylas and Elena Papanastasiou, also points out that the idea of empowerment, can not only have different dimensions, but can also be operationalised in educational practice in many different ways. He points out that the two key features of the concept, namely the ability to control various aspects of one's professional life and participation in decision-making, which are central to the functioning of the educational community, illustrate the contradiction at the heart of the idea of empowerment. The first concerns teachers' autonomy and the second their participation in decision-making. Autonomy, as the author emphasises, means the freedom to make decisions unconstrained by the views of other interested groups (such as, for example, the governing body, the management, parents, students), who may also participate in these decision-making processes (Lawson, 2011). In everyday school life, this tension between autonomy and participatory decision-making often takes the form of conflicts between different individuals that make up school communities.

4.2 Empowerment and management

Empowerment is a concept not only analysed and developed in management science, but it is also an idea successfully implemented into management practices in organisations. It is most often referred to the principles of building relationships between employees and managers. It represents an extension of two theoretical currents in management: participative management and work enrichment. The analysis of empowerment as a management strategy or a method requires the consideration of two mutually permeating planes: organisational and psychological. In the organisational perspective, it refers to "a set of purposeful managerial actions and practices that give power, control and authority to subordinates. Psychological empowerment is the perception, the acceptance of being supported, strengthened and subjectified" (Moczydłowska, 2013, pp. 15–23). With this basic distinction in mind, it is worth emphasising that whether empowerment is analysed from an organisational or psychological perspective, it concerns employees and power relations in the workplace.

In the context of management, it is important to identify the objectives of applying empowerment strategies. Among the basic ones, the building of collaborative culture seen as a starting point for innovation and stability is indicated (Moczydłowska, 2013, pp. 15–23). In management practice, this means greater employee autonomy. In order to identify the key features of empowerment in relation to the management of organisations, I will refer to the characteristics proposed by Monika Bobzien, which constitute the essential distinguishing features of the concept under discussion. These are as follows:

- participation – empowerment leads to co-participation, which means that it is always carried out with the individuals, groups, institutions concerned in order to support their plans and actions;
- resource-oriented approach – in analyses of workers' competence resources, the focus should not be on deficits, but on the strengths and opportunities of individuals and groups;
- social embedding – a prerequisite for the implementation of capacity-building and agency-oriented activities is, on the one hand, the support of the participants in these processes and, on the other hand, the use of structural and institutional support;
- the style and working method in empowerment-oriented proceedings always focus on development, assistance, cooperation and networking;
- the aim is to expand the possibilities of all participants in the process;
- empowerment is achieved by supporting the development of competences, the redistribution of power and the activation of democratic action among individuals, groups, organisations and communities (Bobzien, 2002, p. 233).

An interesting way to analyse empowerment within management science is also proposed by Taejun Cho and Sue R. Faerman. The authors point to two approaches to analysing this mode of management. The first is structural or relational empowerment, which refers to the reorganisation of management practices. The second is psychological or motivational empowerment, which is aimed at strengthening the potential of individuals and groups (Cho & Faerman, 2010, pp. 33–51). T. Cho and S.R. Faerman pointed out that in structural terms, empowerment is most often seen as a new management alternative describing the meaning of relationships (including power) in the workplace in a different manner. It is also described as a change in management practice that transfers responsibility for decision-making to employees at lower levels of the organisational structure, as a practice of power sharing, as a process of empowering people to influence events, outcomes of actions, and as a redefinition of the meaning of individuals and groups in organisations. The authors also proposed their own definition, in which they define empowerment as "a redefinition of the structure or mode of management in which managers delegate responsibility and information to their subordinates to enable employees to participate in the decision-making process" (Cho & Faerman, 2010, pp. 33–51). This definition integrates two approaches to the attempts to define structural empowerment. In one, the authors emphasise participation as a key element, while others point to the concept of power sharing. The authors proposed a multidimensional model for analysing empowerment in the field of management. They identified three dimensions as fundamental to this concept:

- participatory decision-making,
- performance feedback,
- delegation (Cho & Faerman, 2010, pp. 33–51).

The postulate of participatory decision-making is based on the belief that having an impact on the reality in which one participates is always beneficial and influences changes in attitudes and behaviour, increases the level of satisfaction with the activities performed and reduces the level of resistance and absenteeism. Participatory decision-making is defined as a management process that allocates power and authority among employees by increasing their level of involvement (Cho & Faerman, 2010, pp. 33–51). Another aspect of structural empowerment involves feedback on the effectiveness of actions taken and knowledge sharing. As T. Cho and S.R. Faerman observe, for an employee to be involved in management processes, he or she should receive information from colleagues and superiors, as well as information about the organisation itself. These data help to understand the context of actions taken, the legitimacy of decisions and foster the process of building commitment. Particular importance is given in this context to feedback, which is defined as "information about the current performance or activities of the system used to exercise control over actions in the future" (Cho & Faerman, 2010, pp. 33–51). This means that in structural empowerment, feedback is used to design change or rationalise processes within an organisation. Such an approach causes feedback to be perceived as one of the tools of management. It is assumed that the more an employee is aware of the processes taking place in the organisation and the more reliable and comprehensive knowledge she or he has of their own competences and actions, the more effectively she or he can modify their own attitudes and behaviour. The last distinguished area concerns the delegation of tasks and authority. Some authors see these activities as part of participatory decision-making, while others consider it a separate aspect of structural empowerment (Cho & Faerman, 2010, pp. 33–51). The essence here is to invite interaction and develop individual autonomy.

Analysing the way empowerment is perceived in management, it is possible to identify three basic measures taken in this strategy. The first is motivation, understood as encouraging employees to be more active. The second is management by involvement, understood as engaging employees to take responsibility for improving their working methods. The third is management by delegation, which involves empowering employees to make decisions (Smith J., 2006, p. 8). This is a rather simplistic vision of management but, as Jean Brillman points out, the implementation of these activities requires certain conditions in the organisation. These include the definition of degrees of freedom, limits, decision-making constraints, immediate access to information and new information technologies, the existence of decision-support systems and the possibility of mobilising internal resources (Brilman & Bolesta-Kukułka, 2002, p. 350).

4.3 Empowerment in education

The findings presented above regarding the perception of empowerment as a mode of management in the context of educational practices seem insufficient. Definitions from the field of management science do not sufficiently take into account the complexity of the relationships and dependencies among all stakeholders that make up a school community. Analysing Ricky W. Griffin's classic definition, which describes an organisation "as a group of people who work together in an orderly and coordinated way to achieve a certain set of goals" (Griffin, 1996, p. 35), it is difficult to treat pupils as co-participants in the school community as the cited author defines the organisation. It is also difficult to place parents in the context of this definition. Also the already classic definition by Daniel Katz and Robert L. Kuhn, who see an organisation "as a social system that consists of three elements: organisational roles, the norms sanctioning these roles and the values, i.e. the ideological justifications from which these norms are derived" (Katz & Kahn, 1979, p. 64), does not solve the problem of defining the relationships between all participants not only in the school's everyday life, but also individuals in the school's closer and further environment.

School as such is an organisation and its activities can be analysed according to the criteria ascribed to organisations in the management sciences. This organisational perspective can be successfully used to analyse the relationship between the principal and the teacher, and between the governing body and the principal. The situation becomes more complicated if students and parents are included in these analyses. The complexity of these relationships makes the analysis of dependencies and opportunities for influence and co-determination not only complex, but also multidirectional and multifaceted. Hence, this part of the chapter will present how empowerment can be perceived and applied to social and especially educational practices.

As already emphasised earlier, empowerment as a mode of action has been adopted by different fields of social practice. Among the reasons for the popularity of the concept, Franz Stimmer points to its ethical foundations and action orientation aimed at change, reform, or improvement (Stimmer, 2000, pp. 49–50). An important feature of the empowerment methodology, which enhances its usefulness in social practice, is that it integrates actions on multiple levels. These activities are simultaneously directed at improving the functioning of individuals, groups, organisations and communities. The axiological and teleological underpinnings of the concept are also important. As the cited author notes, the axiological foundations of empowerment derive from concepts related to deficit- and conflict-oriented perspectives and lead to an explicit focus on resource analysis, which is firmly embedded in the ethical and social aspects of the problem. This means that the goals of the activities are mainly defined in terms of self-determination, social justice and democratic participation (Stimmer, 2000, pp. 49–50). In practice, these objectives relate to activities aimed at supporting individuals, groups, organisations and communities so that they acquire the competence, motivation and capacity to solve their own problems and improve their situation. This way of framing assistance emphasises the need to empower the individuals, groups, organisations and communities with whom one works.

In analysing how the concept of empowerment can be used in education, I will refer to the basic levels on which action objectives are designed in this approach. Empowerment is aimed at identifying the deficits and resources that shape a given situation. Their diagnosis may concern: individuals, groups, institutions and the local environment (Stimmer, 2000, pp. 53–56). This division organises the reflection on the applied values of the concept.

Objectives aimed at improving the situation of individuals are linked to a sound diagnosis of resources and deficits. Diagnosis is seen here as a prerequisite for projects of broad pedagogical actions or for specific interventions. Referring to the classical division of developed diagnosis into sub-diagnoses, it is worth emphasising that for work in terms of empowerment, a classification diagnosis is the least valuable. What carries greater value is the diagnosis of meaning, aetiological and prognostic (Paluchowski, 2007, p. 16). Identifying resources and deficits is the basis for the most precise design of offers fostering support or development. The assumption here is that these offers should be tailored to the actual individual needs of the person to be supported. It is worth emphasising that in an educational context, an individual who is being professionally supported is not identified only with a student or possibly his or her parents. This way of thinking also applies to the diagnosis of individual resources of professional teachers and educational management staff. In addition to resources and deficits, the reasons for low activity or inactivity are an important target for diagnostic recognition. If empowerment is to be aimed at co-determination, cooperation and taking responsibility for tasks that the individual can undertake independently, an important aspect is to recognise the lack of motivation to undertake these activities. Data from a diagnosis in this area can, on the one hand, contribute to the individualisation and adaptation of the pedagogical offer and, on the other hand, can facilitate the choice of methods and techniques for working with a particular individual.

In group work, empowerment is applicable to work with families, peer groups, school classes and work teams. The methodology of work in this area is oriented towards the recognition of the group's resources and deficits, so that actions can be planned to transform the group into a team and trigger synergy effects. Diagnosis in this area includes an analysis of group roles, cohesion, norms, developmental phases, leadership and conflicts. In working with the group, emphasis is placed on the appropriate selection of tasks to increase group cohesion and effectiveness. It is important to propose tasks of an additive nature and avoid disjunctive and conjunctive ones (Stimmer, 2000, p. 57). This observation not only applies to work with children and young people, but it is also applicable when designing development offers for boards of education or staff teams. The diagnosis of group resources and deficits also addresses the determinants of group effectiveness. Referring to the concept of the three-dimensional perception of team effectiveness, variables such as team performance, satisfaction of team members and conditions for future cooperation are also analysed (Hackman & Morris, 1975, pp. 45–99).

In the context of the school as an institution, empowerment has very broad implementation possibilities. Those features of the concept which are emphasised in management science are applicable here. In addition to the obvious perspective of analysing relationships within an institution, the material, informational and financial resources that determine the effectiveness of an organisation's functions can be analysed. Empowerment also facilitates reflection on the relationship between the assumed and actual functions of the school. Strategic management and evaluation techniques – both *ex-ante*, formative, and *ex-post* – can be applied here.

The fourth perspective involves the local environment. It has an important, although often underestimated, influence on the functioning of schools. The characteristics of the local environment, i.e. its socio-demographic structure, financial potential, location, infrastructure and traditions, model how educational needs and tasks are interpreted. Local educational policy is that area which, on the one hand, can be a factor for the transmission of educational ideology and, on the other hand, can stimulate or impede initiatives and programmes related to educational goals. The quality and direction of educational policy at the local level and the competence of decision-makers, especially in communicating with other actors in educational processes, can determine the quality and direction of local education.

It is worth emphasising that empowerment in social practices, including education, can be analysed as:
- a state of – enhancement, authorization, growth, a sense of agency, a sense of power and capability, exercising control,
- a process – restoring strength, dignity, control, strengthening competence, giving support, developing skills,

- the purpose of educational and social interventions in a broad sense (Rosalska, 2006).

This way of looking at empowerment makes it possible to see how useful this concept can be for the management of educational processes. It not only makes it possible to direct these processes towards a precisely defined goal, but also to choose appropriate methods for realising this goal. A different way of thinking is proposed by P.-A. Tengland, who indicates that empowerment can be seen from two perspectives – as a goal and as a meaning. In the latter perspective, empowerment can be analysed as a process, a method and an approach. On the other hand, when analysing the perspective in which empowerment is perceived as an objective, the author has operationalised the indicators proving that a state of empowerment has been achieved, or indicate what should be pursued to achieve this state. These include: the ability to control one's own life (individual, family, group or community), a sense of autonomy, knowledge, awareness of development, competence, self-esteem, self-efficacy and self-belief (Tengland, 2008, pp. 77–96). These indicators may be at the same time the variables analysed in studies on the level of democratisation of specific educational institutions, or they may constitute the direction of educational activities aimed at realising the objectives anticipated in this way.

For the considerations undertaken in this publication, an interesting perspective for analysing the possibilities of implementing empowerment in education is that of educational policy. If one assumes that one of the key features of empowerment is sharing power, this task in the context of everyday educational practices seems particularly noteworthy. Power in schools is most often perceived through an analysis of the principal's relationship with other participants of educational processes. However, this is, in the context of educational policy, too narrow a perspective. Leaving aside the issue of analysing the rich proposals for definitions of the category of power formulated in various sciences, I would like to refer to the concept of school governance proposed by Seth Kreisberg (Kreisberg, 1992). It is a concept that explicitly justifies the need for empowerment in education and, at the same time, points out the multifaceted factors inhibiting the process of implementing empowerment in educational practices. The author proposes to reflect on two fundamental issues – how power manifests itself in school everyday life and how it can be used to build and strengthen attitudes related to preparing all members of school life for participation in the wider society. Kreisberg states that power can be understood as domination, but also, under certain conditions, its transformative power can be harnessed. The perception of power in school can be accomplished by analysing how it manifests itself on a continuum stretched between domination and empowerment. Domination, according to the cited author, is a common phenomenon in management. Kreisberg emphasises that the same patterns of domination apply in education as in other institutions (Kreisberg, 1992). These patterns do not only apply to the teacher-pupil relationship, but are also replicated in the relationship between the principal and teachers, between the principal and parents, and between teachers and parents. Empowerment is, in the author's view, the opposition to domination. He uses this concept to describe a new ideology for the perception of power in schools. He defines it "as a process by which people and/or communities reinforce their control or power over their own lives and the decisions that shape those lives" (Kreisberg, 1992).

Empowerment defined in this way can be recognised in psychological terms as a process aimed at building an individual's sense of value, meaning and agency. It can also be used to analyse social processes and actions within specific institutions. In the context of school work, it is a concept that aims to prepare all members of the school community to practice participation. Kreisberg observes, however, that in order to make this postulate a reality, it is necessary to give control and influence to all those involved in the process. This means the necessity of sharing power. This translates not only into sharing the ability to make decisions and having real influence, but also making available the resources that have hitherto been at the sole disposal of the principal. Referring to the work of the precursors of empowerment thinking, Barbara Solomon and Charles Kieffer, Kreisberg draws attention to another condition for the success of empowerment in schools, according to this concept. This includes the competences of the people who make up the school community. After Ch. Kieffer, he calls them participatory competences (Kreisberg, 1992). They are related not only to individual intellectual resources and personality traits, but also to skills, such as defining one's own needs and goals and critically analysing the social and cultural context of the actions taken.

Sharing power also requires sharing responsibility. This means that the people with whom the principal wants to share the power must be willing to accept that, to a limited extent, they will also assume responsibility. Kreisberg makes it clear that people in the school community must be adequately prepared to take on responsibility. The idea of empowerment implies that participants in educational processes have the right to influence and (co)decide. However, insufficient knowledge and skills may become a barrier. When competences for co-determination are recognised as insufficient, opportunities are sought to enhance the potential of individuals, groups or communities. It is an approach that aims to develop, expand capabilities and learn. This perception of participatory competences modifies the perception of educational offers for teachers and other school staff. This modification broadens the profile of desirable teacher competences to include those related to the management of processes carried out in the school community.

The second area to consider when analysing the power relationship in school involves the interests of individual stakeholders. They are defined as all individuals and entities actively involved in the implementation of the project and benefiting from the effects of its implementation, as well as all individuals and organisations whose interests may be affected by its implementation and the outcomes of its implementation (Döbert, 2011, p. 47). This definition can be successfully used to describe and analyse the power relations and conflicts of interest taking place in the school space. Stakeholders can be defined as individuals, groups or institutions that have a relationship with a school because of an underlying interest. These interests may be of different nature – direct or indirect, active or passive, conscious or unconscious, acknowledged or unacknowledged, close or distant in time. This is a particularly interesting theme, as in the context of empowerment it concerns the analysis of power and fields of influence rather than power sharing. This issue is well recognised in analyses of educational management practices. In the context of the purpose of this publication, the school's relationship with the social environment and primary stakeholders will be discussed in the chapter on strategic management.

4.4 Determinants of the implementation of the empowerment concept into educational practice

The concept of empowerment is well described as a management and governance approach. Analyses cover both the assumptions of the concept, its evolution and the conditions for its effectiveness. While in the management sciences this way of thinking about how to build relationships with employees is accepted and implemented, in the field of educational practice it is still a concept treated more like a postulate than everyday school practice. In the final section of this chapter, I will refer to selected categories that can guide and structure the reflection on the determinants of effective introduction of empowerment into educational analyses and practices. I will indicate the conditions related to the axiological foundations of empowerment, the teleological perspective, the methodological perspective and the assumptions from the field of educational policy.

The first perspective is axiological in nature. It is fully justified. As Grzegorz Żuk notes, the word "value", which has its origin in the Latin word *valere*, means 'to be healthy, to be well; to have influence, importance, to be able'. The concept can also be related to *dovalidus*, which means 'strong, powerful, nimble, defensive, influential, effective' (Żuk, 2016, p. 18). These concepts are an important element of the set of categories attributed to the notions of *empowerment* and *empowered*. In relation to education, however, more important than an analysis of the etymology of the two concepts is the reflection on what importance is attributed in educational ideologies to such values as power, freedom or self-determination. It is not the purpose of this chapter to analyse individual educational concepts as a background for assessing the value of the concept of empowerment in educational practices. The primary aim is to point out the relevance of the distinction between declarative and actual values. While declarative values can be deciphered from theoretical studies, pedagogical manifestos, postulates of reformers, concepts of school work prepared for competitions for the position of school principal, statutes and regulations of individual institutions, the decoding of values that shape everyday school practices is much more difficult. The methodologies of organisational culture research, action research, ethnographic research can be used in this regard (see: Cervinkova, 2012). It is important to recognise both practices and artefacts of school everyday life. In terms of practices, it is necessary to recognise ways and channels of communication, decision-making, participation in resources, activities in terms of self-governing structures, spheres of influence and co-determination. Artefacts are also a valuable source of such information as: the organisation of school space and specific classrooms, the way areas are designated for particular groups of the school community, the use of corridor space or the acceptance of individual dress preferences (see: Nalaskowski, 2001, pp. 9–11).

The second perspective is teleological in nature. Questions about the purpose and meaning of education are fundamental here. In the context of empowerment, two important issues are worth emphasising. The first concerns the tension between the emancipatory and adaptive function of education. It is clear that for an adaptive ideology, empowerment will not be a solution that is not only attractive but also acceptable. The second problem area is the tension between goals oriented towards socialisation into community roles and goals oriented towards building and developing the individual's personal resources. In both areas, the tension has the same core – it is the approach to power, influence and self-determination.

Both axiological and teleological perspectives are revealed in educational practices. This methodological sphere of the school's work unmasks the actual rather than the declarative approach to empowerment as a goal and a mode of action. The analysis of these practices can be done both at the micro level by recognising patterns of behaviour in the school classroom, by recognising patterns of teacher-student relationships, and by analysing school artefacts. Observations of relationships between other participants in school life, communication styles, organisational culture can also provide data for analysis. In research on empowerment from a methodological perspective, it is also important to pay attention to solutions related to the planning, implementation and evaluation of the didactic process. A lot of information can be provided by analyses of teaching methods and techniques, the way assessment and feedback are carried out. Solutions such as the flipped classroom or problem-based learning will definitely be closer to the idea of empowerment than teaching based on knowledge transmission.

The last perspective of the analysis of the determinants of the implementation of empowerment into educational practices relates to educational policy, both at the meso and macro level. The systemic framework, most often in the form of legal acts, creates conditions that may or may not be conducive to a culture of empowerment. Decentralisation-oriented solutions will foster the power sharing and responsibility. This is particularly evident through an analysis of the policies of school governing bodies. Public school principals operate within a framework designed by the leading authorities and educational supervision. Depending on how broad this framework is and what the distribution of rights and responsibilities is, principals of individual institutions can design adequate solutions related to the implementation of empowerment. Educational policies can also be interpreted as factors that create a climate conducive to widening the space of freedom combined with responsibility. In the absence of such a climate, undertaking empowerment and self-determination activities may not only be unprofitable, but also risky.

Summarising the above discussion on the determinants of the appeal of the empowerment concept and the potential for its use in everyday educational practices, it is worth emphasising that it is a concept requiring not only knowledge and pedagogical sensitivity, but also courage. Courage refers to the need to confront dominant (at various levels) educational ideologies and beliefs. It is also necessary in the area of power sharing in schools. This is difficult especially in those systems where the responsibility for the pedagogical and educational processes rests solely with the principals.

Małgorzata Rosalska

Chapter V:
Building relationships with the community as part of school management

School as an open system does not function in social vacuum. It is involved in numerous, more or less intense, relationships with various entities from its closer or further environment. These relationships affect the direction and dynamics of the processes carried out at school, and are also important in decision-making. Bearing this in mind, it can be assumed that the management of school tasks with regard to building and maintaining relationships with the social environment belongs to important responsibilities of the headmaster. The quality of their implementation is not only connected with how the institution is perceived in its environment, but also with the ability to use synergies associated with cooperation with individual stakeholders.

The tasks of headmaster are directed both internally and externally. Internal activities concern processes related to teaching, upbringing, care and administration. Externally oriented activities concern building relationships with the closer and further environment, implementing educational policies formulated at the national, regional and local levels, acquiring resources and allies, building the image of the institution, maintaining relations with school stakeholders. Activities undertaken in this area require from the headmaster specific competencies associated with the strategic management of the institution. Competencies related to being a politician, animator, negotiator also seem to be necessary.

This part of the book will identify the elements of social environment within the scope of the headmaster's various interactions, as well as the challenges of strategic management in educational institutions. It will also include a reflection on those aspects of headmaster's work that are related to building the image of school in its social environment and possibilities of using marketing as one of the elements of managing the processes conducted at school.

5.1 Social environment of school

Analyzing the tasks of headmaster connected with managing relations with social environment involves an in-depth diagnosis of the environmental conditions in which school operates. This is due to the complexity of contexts in which individual institutions operate. Recognition of the environment is the primary point of reference for analyzing school activities and educational processes implemented in it. It is viewed broadly, through the prism of identifiable factors that can support or hinder the implementation of typical school processes. The environment can be considered not only as a background for the activities undertaken at school, but also as a factor that models these activities, energizing or hindering them.

The social environment of school includes elements of demographic, economic, natural, technological, political, cultural, legal and technological nature. These are variously organized and called (Hall, 2007, p. 65). These factors can be analyzed in the context of micro, meso and macro environment. Assuming that each school as an element of the educational system is subject to similar macro-environmental influences, especially those of political nature, these factors can clearly differ from one another in micro and meso perspectives. The educational system provides a framework, environment, and context for the implementation of educational processes. The factors inherent in the micro and meso environment condition the direction, quality and dynamics of these processes. At the same time, it is worth noting that these processes do not concern only educational tasks. They are also activities aimed at facilitating the fulfilment of teaching, upbringing and care goals. These processes include, for example, management of resources such as finance, infrastructure or personnel.

Recognizing these factors, their description and analysis, are among the tasks of the headmaster who wants to intentionally shape the relationship between her/his establishment and its environment. In order to accomplish these, he or she can use both non-scenario methods, such as trend extrapolation, as well as numerous scenario methods. The choice of strategy and methodology for this analysis depends on the headmaster's research competence, the characteristics of the environment, and the available data. It is important that the assumptions and goals for building relations with the external environment are based on sound premises. In the context of the work of school and the dynamics of change in the processes that determine its activities, special attention should be paid to scenario-based methods that facilitate predicting the impact of phenomena occurring in the environment and assessing potential risks and potential opportunities that the future may bring (Gierszewska & Romanowska, 2002, p. 76).

External institutions with which school cooperates can be divided into several categories. These include local government units, which constitute the governing body of school, institutions of education system, law enforcement agencies, social welfare institutions, other schools and educational institutions, cultural institutions, clubs and sports facilities, churches and religious associations, businesses and labour market institutions and non-governmental organizations, universities, health care institutions, or media. It is also worth adding to this set the community-specific institutions, such as, for example, fire stations or forestry departments (Hernik, Solon-Lipiński & Stasiowski, 2012, p. 19). This list is not complete, but it illustrates how multifaceted these relationships are. At the same time, it should be noted that the strength of the relationship between school and its environment is differentiated by the permeability of the school's external boundaries. Schools with more permeable boundaries will be more willing to take advantage of the resources inherent in the environment, engage in local initiatives, cooperate with other stakeholders interested in participating in establishing an environment conducive to learning inside and outside school (Dryll, 2021, p. 36).

Cooperation between school and its environment can be analyzed from multiple aspects. Assuming that it can involve both bilateral exchange and unilateral transfer, its diagnosis should take into account such aspects as: the context of establishing cooperation, its content, the basis of cooperation, intensity, efficiency, as well as the direction of resource transfer (Hernik, Solon-Lipiński & Stasiowski, 2012, pp. 17–18). This means that each school individually designs the scope and intensity of these relationships. Reasonable identification of institutional resources and allies in the environment of the institution is worth pointing out as the key task in the context of the headmaster's activities in the discussed area. Such an in-depth diagnosis can be the basis for cooperation projects, which will be oriented towards the attainment of the most important goals from the point of view of a particular school.

The prospect of the relationship between school and its environment is interesting from the perspective of designing educational policies. Lorraine M. McDonnell points out that institutions, along with public interest and ideology, are one of the basic elements of projects in this regard (McDonnell, 2009, p. 57). The institutional dimension integrates thinking in legal and administrative terms. Analyzing education policy from the institutional perspective is also important because it is the institutions that define the framework for implementing educational policy, and thus influence its implementation and effectiveness. What is important for the quality of school functioning is the saturation of the environment with institutions that support school in achieving its goals. Of particular importance here is the availability of institutions providing therapeutic, specialized assistance and support in the field of prevention. The available range of offers in the field of social assistance and cultural animation is important as well.

Analysis of the scope of relations, their direction and dynamics is also relevant in the context of the second element identified by the quoted author, namely, the public interest.

Education is a space where not only the interests of direct participants in educational processes converge, but also the interests of representatives of the school social environment. In the context of building relations with the environment, the interests articulated by the governing and controlling bodies of schools are particularly vital. The most important forces of the social environment, which exert a multidirectional influence on schools and their leaders and directly or indirectly express their expectations towards school activities, can include such stakeholders as the state and its bodies, social groups (political parties, churches and religious associations, associations and foundations, trade unions), the media, as well as academic and scientific circles. When analyzing the impact of the external environment, it is also worth considering the closer, local environment. It is at this level that arrangements for the school network and human resources policies implemented by governing bodies are articulated and negotiated. It can be assumed that while stakeholders from the macro zone put forward postulates that are mainly ideological in nature, the local level is dominated by economic and social interests identified with the individual needs of particular groups of local influence.

5.2 Strategic management

While an in-depth diagnosis of the resources and allies in the school social environment is important in the context of planning development directions and fundraising, strategic management can be considered a way of thinking and acting aimed at building synergistic relationships between the institution and its environment. Two basic phases can be identified in the process of strategic management. The first is strategic planning, which implies cognitive activities, goal setting and strategy development; the second is strategy implementation, which includes activities resulting from strategic planning, i.e. strategic administration and control (Przyszczypkowski & Solarczyk-Ambrozik, 2002, p. 7). Thus, the starting point for the development of educational strategies is a diagnosis that takes into account data regarding the analyzed processes and phenomena and the external factors that condition them.

Strategic management is defined as "a management process focused on developing and implementing strategies that foster a higher degree of compatibility between the organization and its environment and the achievement of strategic goals". According to the concept proposed by R.W. Griffin, every strategy includes four basic areas: scope, resource deployment, distinctive competence and synergy. This approach can also be successfully applied to strategic management in education. The areas indicated by Griffin are suitable for the analysis of management processes in education, they allow us to analyze the processes carried out at the interface between school and its environment (Griffin, 2021, p. 206).

Scope defines the set of markets in which the organization will compete. In the context of school, defining the scope means recognizing the key characteristics of the target group of educational services and the characteristics of the operating environment of the institution, for which it designs an offer not only didactic, but also educational, caring and sometimes social. Determination of scope can take the form of an in-depth environmental diagnosis, the purpose of which will not only be a description, but, first and foremost, the identification of needs and factors supporting or hindering their realization. Identifying the scope can also be relevant to the design of marketing procedures of school or other educational institution.

Another area of strategic management involves the resource deployment, i.e. "how the organization distributes its resources in the areas in which it competes" (Griffin, 2021, p. 234). The way in which resources are managed, how they are allocated and how they are used applies to all groups of resources managed by the school headmaster. The analysis of resource deployment can involve both the ways of using school infrastructure and managing employees. Thinking in the perspective of strategic management makes it possible to diagnose the allocation of resources in the context of the efficiency of conducted activities, cost-effectiveness or optimization of processes. In this context, one can also think about the ways in which school can use resources inherent in its environment or use its own resources for the benefit of the local community or in terms of increasing its own financial reserves. Such thinking is more common in the meso perspective of educational policy design, but can also be used in the management of individual facilities or in projects involving cooperation between schools and institutions supporting their work within a single governing body.

The third area is distinctive competence. For educational processes, it defines what distinguishes the school, what it is particularly good at, what it specializes in, what gives it a competitive advantage. The starting point for a discussion of distinctive competence is always an analysis of the school social environment, the offerings of schools competing for students in the same environment, and the diagnosis of school resources and capabilities. In a situation where the school has no competition in its local community, the need to develop a distinctive competence is not significant. The situation is different in highly competitive environments. This occurs when several schools compete for students in the environment of clear demographic crisis. Another example could involve competition between high schools or vocational training schools, or between kindergartens with a similar territorial range. Defining the distinctive competence of an institution is a creative task on the one hand, requiring intensive conceptual work. On the other hand, it is a process that requires in-depth diagnosis and analysis, since the identification of a category that distinguishes an organization from others in the long run will condition the directions of its development, investment and marketing strategy.

The last area of strategic management identified by R.W. Griffin is synergy. It is defined as "the way in which various areas of organisational activity complement or support one another" (Griffin, 2021, p. 235). At the school level, synergy should apply to the implementation of didactic, educational and caring processes. It is the opposite of competition. It is based on the assumption that cooperation, coordination of activities is supposed to enhance efficiency. The mechanism of synergy can be used in the management of individual schools, but it can also be one of the reference points for designing educational policy at the local or regional level. Adopting a way of viewing and analyzing educational resources in such a way as to harness their potential for building social capacity can unleash synergy in a broader perspective. An important aspect of synergy-oriented activity is building a culture of cooperation, assistance, and pursuit of common goals. In the field of education, this goal is also to build community social capital.

Taking into account the broad context of analyzing educational processes serves as prevention against excessive focus on indicators directly related to the analyzed institution or its local environment. Most often these involve economic and demographic indicators. Introducing the need to consider the social and cultural context into the analysis can open up the perspective for designing changes aimed not only at optimizing costs, but also at equalizing social opportunities, supporting underprivileged groups, preventing school failures or building a civil society. The local context reveals the needs in this area and makes meeting them realistic. An important point of reference are local resources – financial, material, human or information. The diagnosis is also performed as to whether the selected tasks are not carried out by too many entities, whether the organization can be optimized, and the infrastructure better utilized. It is at this level of strategic management that decisions are made regarding reorganization and outsourcing the selected services.

In the context of building relationships between school and its social environment, a diagnosis of the organisation itself is also important. However, this is not just a diagnosis of a descriptive-evaluative nature. It is oriented towards demonstrating the relationship between the way the organisation functions, its effectiveness and the conditions of the environment in which the school operates. Most often researchers refer to SWOT analysis at this level. It is a popular analytical technique. Its advantage consists in its simple and structured form. In educational research, it is applicable to identifying resources in the context of planned activities and vision for school development.

5.3 Building relationships with environment

The school belongs to the structure of institutions that implement goals of local communities. It is an element of a broader system. It is impossible to analyze the course of school management without taking into account the processes taking place at the interface between the school and its environment, or even processes taking place in other entities, the consequences of which have a direct or indirect influence on the daily practices in school. In this context, the headmaster is a politician whose task is to collaborate, mediate, negotiate, build relationships, tap into the potential of local community and animate initiatives.

Building relationships with the school social environment can be carried out in different manners. In the literature, authors propose various models for analyzing this process. For the purposes of this publication, two of them will be mentioned. The first model proposed by Chris Huxham includes four ways of building relationships with the environment. These are: networking, coordination, collaboration and partnership. The first way, based on networking is simple and does not require commitment of resources and changes in the organizational culture. It is based on cooperation which consists in exchanging information and the task of school is to find proper partners and establish possibly most effective channels of information exchange. Coordination is a more complex form. It involves realization of common goals through joint action. This means the need to develop and adjust trans-unit strategies for action. The organization of work, distribution of resources, perception of goals and hierarchy of priorities require adjustment in this situation. Cooperation based on coordination strives for synergy as the primary effect of joint action. The third way of working together involves collaboration. It is based on joint planning and organizing activities. Changes in organizational culture are more advanced here than for coordination, but they are not permanent and cover the duration of the joint task or project. The last way of cooperation identified by Huxham is based on partnership understood as trust, support, joint learning. This is the most advanced form of cooperation (Huxham, 2003, pp. 401–423).

The invoked author also pointed out an interesting concept of analyzing inter-organizational cooperation. He indicated the tension between two perspectives of analyzing the topic. The first focuses on benefits. The concept of *collaborative advantage* emphasizes synergy as the goal of cooperation. It assumes that in order to obtain a real benefit from cooperation, something must be achieved that could not be achieved by any of the organizations acting alone. The other focuses on difficulties and losses. The concept of *collaborative inertia* takes into account the problem of negligible, slow or insufficient effects of cooperation (Huxham, 2003, pp. 401–423). Analyzing both various ways of understanding the concept of cooperation and the practices in this area, the author identified four basic themes of cooperation. These are the categories that can provide a useful canvass for analyzing collaboration between schools and their social environment, such as: goals, power, trust, and membership structures.

The first of these involves common goals. It is assumed that the basis of joint projects are common or concerted goals, and that they energize the activities of collaborating entities. In educational practice, however, it is worth noting the imprecision and sometimes even discrepancy between the declared and actual goals. An important aspect is also the hidden agenda not only of school, but also of the institutions surrounding it. The risk of dissonance of goals is particularly pronounced where the basis of the activities of individual organizations consists in ideological assumptions based on a strong axiological message. The second theme is power, its exercise and distribution. Of particular interest for the practice of collaboration management is the identification of the *points of power* that form the *power infrastructure* for collaboration (Huxham & Beech, 2008). Many of these occur at micro level and are so subtle that they are not even perceived by the partners as an area of governance. Huxham indicates here such elements as the name of the project, how partners are selected for collaboration, how meetings are organized and moderated. It is worth noting that the infrastructure of power is not static. The activity of individual partners can change due to the phase of the project, as well as the prevailing goals. Another theme regarding cooperation involves trust. Although the existence of trust-based relationship between partners would be an ideal situation, according to Huxham, it is more often suspicion rather than trust that lies at the root of various types of cooperation.

Often partners do not have the opportunity to choose other people and institutions with whom they want to work. Either imposed (local, regional, macro) policies dictate who must be a partner, or the pragmatics dictates which partners are needed for specific tasks. This means that especially at the beginning of the collaboration – the focus should be on building trust between partners. The author points to two factors that are important for starting a trusting relationship. The first concerns the formation of expectations about the future of the collaboration. If it is to be based on reputation or past behaviour then trust pays off for all parties involved. The second starting point relates to risk taking. The argument is that partners must trust each other enough to be willing to take risks in order to initiate collaboration. If both factors are viable, the research seems to suggest that trust can be built by starting with modest but realistic goals that are likely to be attained, thus reinforcing attitudes of trust and thereby gaining a basis for more ambitious collaboration.

The fourth theme is membership structures. Huxham describes them through three aspects: ambiguity, complexity and dynamics. Ambiguity refers to the partners' knowledge of the collaborating organisations, i.e. their goals, objectives, responsibilities and justifications for building cooperation. Complexity defines the number and variety of arrangements and the hierarchy of tasks assigned to each organisation. Dynamics, on the other hand, refers to the rate of change in the structure, its stabilisation through trade-offs. It is worth emphasising that the factors energizing the transformation of the cooperation structure involve both external influences, especially those related to changes in the law or in local policy assumptions, but also the aspirations and actions taken by individual collaborating participants.

The fifth and final theme is leadership, which refers to shaping and implementing the collaboration policy and agenda. Huxham an Vangen (Huxham & Vangen, 2000, pp. 1159–1175) identify two important issues in this area. The first regards the media through which leadership is delivered, and the authors argue that structures and processes are as important in driving agendas as the participants involved in collaboration. The second aspect concerns leadership actions that are directed at nurturing collaboration, such as motivating, encouraging and empowerment. At the same time, they point to destructive actions based on manipulation, politicking and other ethically questionable behaviour.

The second model, or rather a typology of models of cooperation between schools and institutions from the social environment, was developed by Roman Dorczak on the basis of research on collaboration in preventive and educational activities in several dozen Polish schools. The author distinguished five models of schools entering into inter-organisational relationshis (Dorczak, 2012, p. 319). The first is the negative cooperation model. In this model, the transfer of benefits is one-sided, with one institution pursuing its own goals at the expense of the other party. Behaviours such as the exploitation of tangible, intellectual and informational resources are engaged here, often without the consent and knowledge of the partner. The second model is the linear collaboration model, also referred to as the "hot potato" model. It involves successive institutions delegating a task or problem to one another. This is particularly relevant for difficult, unusual situations that school is unable or unwilling to deal with. The case is then referred to more specialised institutions. The next one, the dominance model, occurs when the scope of collaboration, its rules and its course are determined by one of the partners. It differs from the negative collaboration model by the fact that the dominated party is aware of its situation and accepts this treatment because it perceives some benefits to it. The fourth, the parallel action model, is characterised by momentariness, occasionality and sometimes randomness. Sometimes it is only a mock collaboration resulting from formal requirements related to the implementation of a project or raising funds. The last, and as noted by the author of the cited typology, the least frequent model is partnership collaboration. At each stage, partners work together, develop goals and concepts. Activities are jointly planned, organised and implemented. Developed changes or solutions affect all partners and are implemented by all partners. These activities are not random and their effectiveness triggers synergy effect.

The typologies of different models of inter-organisational collaboration presented in this part of the work can provide guidance for headmasters not only in designing collaboration with individual institutions from the closer or further social environment. These models can also be used as a basis for evaluation projects, both those already undertaken and those planned. The evaluation of activities conducted together with institutions from the school social environment can be based on a comparison of specific activities within the models mentioned above. Even if one assumes that pure forms of these models are rarely found in school practice, it is worth recognising their essential features. Designing the evaluation in this way, especially ex-ante, can facilitate and deepen the reflection on whether a particular project, or an offer of cooperation is beneficial in the context of other goals of priority importance to the school.

5.4 Educational marketing

Public relations activities are one of the elements of managing an organisation, including a school. They are an essential element in building school image in its immediate environment. Assuming that fostering public relations represents a management function of a continuous and planned nature, through which the school gains the understanding, sympathy and support of those in whom it is interested now or may be interested in the future, it can be considered that the conscious use of this function is one of the basic tasks of a leader of the school community.[6] Researching opinions about the school, building and disseminating the image, taking care of its coherence and clarity are the tasks of a headmaster who wants to intentionally influence relations with his or her school social environment. In relation to schools, public relations oriented activities constitute also an element of promotion and a marketing tool. In the context of the topic of this section, however, we will focus on activities concerning the positioning of school in the local community. These are primarily aimed at building and

---

6 See: PR definition according to IPRA https://www.ipra.org/member-services/pr-definition/.

maintaining the school's prestige, attracting more pupils or attracting pupils with a particular aptitude profile.

Prestige, understood as social respect, is created in the environment. It has a strongly hierarchical meaning, which becomes particularly significant in communities rich in educational institutions addressing their offer to the same target groups. The presence of prestige is evidenced by behaviours and evaluations directed at individuals, groups, institutions and other "objects" submitted to social evaluation (Domański, 2019, p. 188). In the process of building relationships with the school environment, actions can be taken to shape assessments of the offers and processes undertaken at school. Given that public relations is regarded as a continuous and planned activity, it is the task of the headmaster and his/her team to develop not only the desired image of the school, but also the strategy to achieve and promote it. This is a multi-stage process requiring creative collaboration. At this point, it is worth mentioning the stages of strategic public relations planning proposed by Roland D. Smith. The author identified the following 9 steps:
1. Analyzing the Situation
2. Analyzing the Organization
3. Analyzing the Public
4. Setting Goals and Objectives
5. Creating Action and Response Strategies
6. Developing the Message Strategy
7. Selecting Communication Tactics
8. Implementing the Strategic Plan
9. Evaluating the Strategic Plan (Smith R.D., 2021).

Even a cursory analysis of these stages indicates how elaborate and complex this process is. In the context of school management, it is worth highlighting activities related to the analytical, research sphere. Projects related to promoting the school image in its social environment should be preceded by a reliable diagnosis of both its potential and its perception in the environment. It is important that public relations projects are anchored in reliable and current data, and not just in the vision or projection of the aspirations of managers. In the set of activities proposed above, the first three stages that precede the formulation of goals relate to diagnosis. This includes the analysis of the situation, the organisation and the target group. As well as being broad, it should also be relevant and reliable. And this, in turn, raises questions about the competence of headmasters in designing and implementing research as well as analysing and interpreting the results. The second aspect, whose importance needs to be emphasised in designing public relations, is that of planning and process. Managing relationships with the school social environment requires planning not only the message with the content to be promoted, but also communication strategies. What is important here is the choice of communication channels and the selection of specific tools.

The marketing of educational services has a unique character. This is due to both the organisational context and the characteristics of the service itself. On the one hand, educational services are universal, accessible and free of charge; on the other hand, they are subject to marketing processes. On the one hand, there is an abundance of public schools, while on the other, private educational service providers operate on the market as entrepreneurs focused on multiplying profits. The characteristics of educational services that determine the choice of marketing tools include the intangible nature of the service, the impossibility of acquiring ownership, diversity, inseparability and non-sustainability (Hall, 2007, pp. 121–122; see: Pluta-Olearnik, 2006, p. 33). Furthermore, services provided in schools have additional characteristics that demonstrate their uniqueness: they are interdisciplinary, complex, and difficult to evaluate (Hall, 2007, p. 123). This makes it necessary for marketing activities to be tailored to the characteristics of the services to be promoted, while at the same time targeted at precisely defined objectives. Furthermore, marketing of educational services can also be attributed the characteristics of marketing activities undertaken in other non-commercial institutions. These include:
- multiplicity of objectives,
- the overriding nature of social objectives,
- independence of the pursuit of activities from material gain,
- high dependence on external funding,
- intangible nature of the offer,
- diversity of consumers,
- social pressure,
- dual management (Garbarski, Rutkowski & Wrzosek, 2000, pp. 664–665).

These last three points in particular seem to play a special role in the context of school marketing activities. The diversity of consumers is very intense here. Marketing messages are formulated both to the inside of the institution and to the outside. The obvious recipients are pupils and their parents. However, these messages are also designed for actors in the wider school environment: local community, supervisory authority, governing body and for other schools competing in the area. A factor shaping the direction of marketing activities is also social pressure resulting from the social and educational objectives of school activities on the one hand, and from the way they are publicly funded on the other. The pressure of the leading authorities to promote particular values or activities can be a factor that strongly models the marketing concept proposed by headmasters of individual schools.

This perception of marketing makes it one of the primary tools for managing the relationships between school and its environment. According to Philip Kotler, important benefits of using marketing in educational services include better performance in achieving the school mission, higher levels of student satisfaction, more effective acquisition of marketing resources, and higher efficiency of market activity (Pluta-Olearnik, 2006, p. 30). It is also worth noting that marketing pursuits can be seen from different perspectives. It can be understood as a way of thinking and acting, as a tool for influencing the school environment and as part of an organisational management strategy and decision-making related to its activities (Garbarski, Rutkowski & Wrzosek, 2000, p. 29).

In the context of using marketing tools from the perspective of managing the relationship between school and its environment, relationship marketing is of particular importance. It is defined as an integrated effort to identify, maintain, and build up a network with individual consumers and to continuously strengthen the network for the mutual benefit of both sides, through interactive, individualized and value-added contacts over a long period of time (Shani & Chalasani, 1992, pp. 33–42). This concept of marketing was proposed in the 1980s as a response to the results of research and analysis of customer relationship combined with a strategic orientation in the approach to marketing activities (Seliga & Woźniak, 2014, p. 235). Relationship marketing (RM) is a well-refined, 30-year-old concept first published in *Harvard Business Review* in 1983 (Surej & De Villiers, 2022). Most definitions of relationship marketing emphasise the need to build a connection with a customer. With regard to school, this will not only be a student and his or her parent, but also people and institutions in the social environment. Several common elements characteristic of relationship marketing definitions are noticeable in the literature. These are:
1. Customer orientation.
2. Collection and processing of customer data.
3. Individualisation of customer approach.
4. Feedback communication with customers.
5. Striving for customer loyalty by treating customers as partners (Seliga & Woźniak, 2014, p. 241).

These characteristics also make this type of marketing highly useful in the field of education. Marketing tools are used to build and maintain relationships with individuals for whom school works and with whom it cooperates in achieving its educational and social goals. In the sphere of educational services, the concept of relationship marketing acquires particular significance both because of the relationships that arise in a situation of direct dialogue between school employees and students, their parents, representatives of institutions located in the local environment, and due to the relationships within the school. It is also worth emphasising that relationship marketing fosters the formation and deepening of lasting bonds and connections, also in the long term. For schools operating in specific local communities, this is important for the process of building prestige, reputation and school traditions.

Surej and Rouxel point out that in the field of education, four elements are particularly important in relationship marketing: trust, commitment, service quality and technology adoption (Surej & De Villiers, 2022). They distinguish three dimensions in trust: contractual trust, competence trust and goodwill trust. Contractual trust refers to the belief that the educational institution will abide by the contractual terms and provide the promised quality of education. Competence trust refers to the capacity of the school to deliver the promised services effectively and reliably. Goodwill trust indicates to the recipient of a marketing message that school acts in good faith for the benefit of students and their families.

As for the next dimension, the authors point to three types of commitment. These include normative commitment, affective commitment and continuance. Normative commitment refers to feelings of reciprocity and obligation in relationships. Affective commitment indicates students' emotional attachment to the institution, while continuance refers to the state of attachment that students and their parents cognitively experience after realising the benefits or losses incurred if the relationship with the institution is terminated (Surej & De Villiers, 2022).

The third element identified by the researchers is the quality of the services provided. In the context of schools, this quality is determined not only by academic performance of individual students, but also by the organisation of the processes carried out at school: didactic, educational and caring ones. In their analyses of tertiary education, they indicated that the quality of services is assessed through the prism of four characteristics: teacher involvement, interaction in the learning process, personalisation of interactions and collaboration (Surej & De Villiers, 2022). Although these data refer to tertiary education, it can be assumed that they will also shape the perception of the quality of school activities at other levels. This is an important guideline for those managing the marketing policy in schools. It is important not only to show specific activities, but to situate them in the perspective of values that are a priority for the target group.

The last element identified by the authors is technology adoption. The computerisation of school, its digital resources, the use of information technology in the learning process can be effectively used for marketing. The image of school as a modern institution using the latest developments in information technology can be used in building school identity. However, it is also worth noting that technological solutions can be an effective tool for building relationships between school, its staff and the target audience of marketing messages. The potential for the application of individual tools, such as, for example, e-mail, social networking sites, the school website, video conferencing, should be analysed as part of the design of the overall school marketing policy.

Summarising the content presented in this part of the book, it is worth emphasising that activities of the headmaster aimed at building relationships with the immediate and distant environment belong to the basic tasks in the scope of school management and, to a broader extent, are part of the micro-policy of individual schools. The ability to build relationships, develop and foster them represents an important element of the headmaster's competence profile in modern school. However, it should not be forgotten that the basis for all public relations and marketing activities at school should be an in-depth and reliable diagnosis. Research into the needs and expectations of the target group, an analysis of the organisation current image and an evaluation of the activities undertaken so far – their effectiveness and relevance, constitute important tasks, which should not be overlooked when designing marketing policy of the organisation. This means that in the process of building good relationships with the social environment, the headmaster must not only be a visionary and strategist, but also an attentive, reflective observer of the school reality and the social factors that model its daily functioning.

Agnieszka Cybal-Michalska

Chapter VI:
Leadership versus management – skills accumulation and integrity

6.1 Leadership versus management – similarities, differences, contemporary issues and challenges

Management and leadership are two constructs whose semantic scopes overlap thus contributing to problems with the definitional credo. Leadership and management as entities are complementary, but undoubtedly represent two different concepts (Mahmood, Muhammad & Bashir, 2012, p. 513).

The perception of the terms "leadership" and "management" can assume different semantic orderings. It is possible to treat theses terms as synonyms and use them interchangeably, which can be found in the literature. It is also possible to encounter the approach to the distinguished constructs as extreme opposites, recognising that one cannot be a good manager and a leader at the same time. Most positions treat management and leadership separately with the view that an individual can navigate both (Ricketts, 2009, p. 1).

When addressing this topic, it is worth emphasising that Kotter's distinction between the domains in question is fundamental to understanding what management and leadership mean today. Leadership, which, according to the author, should be considered a construct with a long tradition (developed over the last hundred years) is clearly linked to the industrial revolution. Although the distinctions between the constructs are clear, suffice it to say that, while different, they cannot exist completely separately (Mahmood, Muhammad & Bashir, 2012, p. 513). Against the backdrop of these dilemmas, some questions arise: do leaders and managers have the same role and can an organisation have only leaders or only managers? The answer that comes to mind is the postulate that an efficient organisation should have both leaders and managers. Kotterman adds that in fact an organisation needs a few great leaders and many first-class managers (Bohoris & Vorria, 2007, p. 2). However, by engaging in capturing not universals but specific elements, many theoreticians share Kotter's perspective on the differences between management and leadership. Bennis and Nanus define management as the completion of tasks and mastery of procedures. To lead, on the other hand, is to influence others and create visions for change. In Rost's view, management is one-way guidance, while leadership is a relationship based on multi-directional influence. Consequently, as Zaleznik points out, management and leadership require different types of people. Nevertheless, as clearly emphasised above, these two spheres also overlap; when managers engage in influencing a group of employees to achieve their goals, one can then already speak of leadership. Equally, when leaders engage in aspects such as planning, organising or controlling, they are acting as managers (Ricketts, 2009, p. 2). It is worth noting here that organising is defined as "the logical grouping of activities and resources" whereas controlling is defined as "observing an organisation's progress towards its goals" (Griffin, 2004, pp. 10 and 11). The originality of the reflections proposed is evidenced by the words of K. Matsushik. The distinguished company founder argues that management and leadership are inseparable. In his view, "a leader cannot just delegate management issues to others; instead of separating management from leadership, we should treat managers as leaders and understand leadership as management well executed" (Mintzberg, 2013, p. 26). It becomes an analytical necessity to recognise the distinctive nature of the constructs in question, but also to recognise their "systemic" nature. According to J.P. Kotter, managers are people who are assigned tasks and achieve the desired goals through the key functions such as planning, organising, hiring, problem solving and exercising control. Leaders, on the other hand, set a goal, select a team of people, motivate and inspire. A leader is someone who is flexible, innovative, inspiring to others, courageous and independent. In a nutshell: a leader has a soul, passion and creativity, while a manager has a mind, rational thinking and perseverance (Bohoris & Vorria, 2007, p. 2).

The environmental context of leadership and management also becomes a source of attraction for theoretical considerations. Faced with challenges of the contemporary world and the reality subject to permanent fluctuation, the need for "dynamic management" is postulated, which means, as J.A.F. Stoner, R.E. Freeman, D.R. Gilbert emphasise, that "in today's world, many organisations particularly value managers who also have leadership skills" (Stoner, Freeman & Gilbert, 2001, p. 454). After all, leaders influence the environment and, through social practice, change the structure by three types of action: setting the organisation's values, goals and norms as well as business concepts and strategies and recruiting personnel (Sharma & Jain, 2013, p. 313).

6.2 Personality of a manager versus personality of a leader

The title of the subsection suggests that it is possible to distinguish a set of innate personality traits that will be associated with management or leadership functions and their high effectiveness. However, it is difficult to agree with such a view. A person is not born a manager or a leader, but becomes one. Therefore, it would be more appropriate to speak of managerial and leadership qualities by referring to character traits, according to the psychological view that character consists of what is innate and what is acquired (through one's own activity and the activity of others), with the advantage of the latter. Thus, the essence of managerial and leadership experience is emphasised, and an attempt is made to identify the behavioural traits of effective managers and leaders in order to eventually distinguish management and leadership styles.

The phenomenon of management can be analytically and interpretatively approached from different theoretical perspectives with different conceptual assumptions. One view is to recognise that we are all managers because we manage our finances, time, careers and interpersonal relationships. However, we do not tend to think of ourselves as "managers" and of the activities we undertake as "management". Nonetheless, when we use these concepts in relation to organisations, they become more complex and require a description and exploration of the theoretical underpinnings of management (Darr, 2011, p. 7).

The considerations regarding the separate grouping of assertions about managers and leaders can be based on the notion that management is directed towards maintaining the status quo (transactional by nature), while leadership is visionary and dynamic (transformational by nature) (Darr, 2011, p. 8).

The logic of managerial skills, roles and competences can be structured by pointing to the following: *technical skills* (the ability to use management methods, procedures and techniques. This may include competencies within a specialized field, analytical ability, or the ability to use appropriate tools and techniques. As managers become more experienced, these become less important); *conceptual skills* (the mental capacity to see situations holistically and to treat them as an instrumental whole. This involves the ability to work with ideas and concepts, to focus on ideas. It is particularly important to anticipate the consequences of a decision or non-decision. The importance of the distinguished skills increases with seniority of the manager); *interpersonal skills* (they are connected with cooperation with others, understanding, motivating and leading in the workplace. These skills allow the manager to assist a group of employees to achieve a goal or complete a task. These skills gradually lose their importance with the seniority of the manager) (Darr, 2011, pp. 9–10).

The issue of managerial work can also be approached through the lens of the roles performed. Darr distinguished the following roles: *interpersonal roles* (roles of symbolic guides, leaders and coordinators are rooted in the power of managers); *information roles* (information roles are particularly important in more complex organisations requiring effective communication. Access to information is a measure of power. Thus, less self-confident managers tend to accumulate information, disclosing it rather reluctantly, in order to strengthen their position); *decision-making roles* (a special place is ascribed to negotiation as these are activities that managers perform on a daily basis); *the designer role* (designing various components of the organisation); *the strategist role* (refers to suggesting the direction of the organisational focus, so that the organisation can address challenges and opportunities posed by the external environment); *the leader role* (the leader role is influenced by the execution of the strategist and designer roles) (Darr, 2011, pp. 9–10).

The issue under discussion is reflected in the considerations regarding managerial competences. In addition to skills and roles, managers need to develop the following competencies: *conceptual* (these are analogous to role and conceptual skills. Low-level managers and middle-level managers use conceptual competence to understand how their work relates to the organisation as a whole, and to understand the interrelationships within their area of responsibility. Senior managers use their ability to anticipate the consequences of decisions, or lack thereof); *technical* (they enable managers to do their job more effectively, and to manage work of the departments for which they are responsible more efficiently. Managers without technical knowledge need to put a great deal of effort into understanding the basics of the specialised activities for which they are responsible, as well as to understand the operation of the organisation in general); *interpersonal* (these require managers to have interpersonal skills and the ability to collaborate. These are necessary to manage others effectively); *political* (these mean understanding and being able to work with local or state authorities); *commercial* (economic success requires organisations to create economic exchanges that provide value for both parties. Managers need to create and maintain the right environment that facilitates such exchanges. This requires a good business orientation, but also a human approach. Many non-profit organisations concentrate on spreading the good, but at the same time neglect the fact that the organisation also needs to be managed, like any other business); *governing* (these involve working with the board to establish a vision for the organisation, use resources, run the organisation and be accountable to shareholders) (Darr, 2011, pp. 9–10). All of the above skills, competencies and roles are important for effective management and necessary at different levels of management within an organisation. It is therefore not surprising that they are also useful for effective leadership, although in a slightly different context (Ricketts, 2009, p. 3). Characteristics of effective leaders include: dominance (willingness to take charge; self-confidence; extroversion), dutifulness (drive to succeed, energy, initiative), social competence (expressive attention, ability to listen, little need to be liked), and a sense of internal control (optimism, resilience; perseverance). In addition, it is highlighted that effective leaders tend to have higher than average intelligence – especially reasoning and memory (Kilian, 2007, p. 4).

Northouse's comparison of management and leadership competencies indicates that there are clear discrepancies between these concepts. Following the author, it is recognised that management introduces order and consistency (planning, budgeting, creating a calendar, allocating resources, hiring staff, creating structure, undertaking placements, setting policies and procedures, controlling and solving problems, motivating staff, generating creative solutions, taking corrective measures) and leadership focuses on change and dynamism (setting direction, creating and interpreting vision, establishing strategy, seeking commitment, creating teams, motivating and inspiring, energising, empowering subordinates) (Ricketts, 2009, p. 3).

According to J. Kotterman, the most important differences between leaders and managers relate to the three dimensions of activity framed in processual terms. In the process of "creating a vision", a manager plans the budget; develops subsequent steps of the process and sets deadlines, displays an impersonal attitude towards the vision and goals. On the other hand, a leader sets the direction and develops the vision, also develops strategic plans and implements the vision, shows a passionate attitude towards the vision and goals. In the process of "developing people and networking", a manager is responsible for the organisation and for personnel policies, maintains structure, delegates responsibility, distributes authority, implements the vision, establishes policies and procedures needed to achieve the vision, limits employee choices. In contrast, a leader communicates vision, mission and direction, influences the formation of coalitions, teams and partnerships that understand and accept the vision, enhances the choice made by employees. As regards the process of "vision implementation", a manager: controls the process, identifies problems, solves problems, monitors results and takes a low-risk approach to solving problems. In turn, a leader: motivates and inspires, energises employees to overcome obstacles on the road to change, takes a high-risk approach to solving problems. In the process of "vision outcomes", a manager controls the order and predictability in the implementation of the vision, presents expected results to management and other stakeholders, whereas a leader promotes useful and dramatic changes, such as new products or new approaches to improving working relationships (Bohoris & Vorria, 2007, pp. 2–3).

In further considerations, it is worth noting the crystallisation of manager's or leader's identity. Consequently, the studies on this issue have resulted in the introduction of the following concepts: "assuming and creating a role and identity, self-concept, self-image, merging a role with a person, role distance, presentation of self, casting in a role" (Hałas, 1998, p. 356). It is in the process of interaction and communication that new meanings are created and the situation is defined. In these considerations, the managerial or leadership situation also highlights the way in which the self is experienced in interaction, discovering the meaning of "difference" for the subject identity crystallisation (be it a manager or a leader) as a result of the permanent interaction between the individualised self and social environment. Individuals, as B. G. Glaser and A. L. Strauss emphasise, "'wander' between the statuses they co-create in their collaboration and interaction with others, reciprocally gaining confirmation of their own self-concepts and their own identity." (Rokicka, 1992, p. 116). This important insight into the subjective aspects of a manager's or leader's career, such as the individual status, self-concept, social reactions to role-playing, means that individuals are not captured as a "stable entity". The self, which is relational and arises in the processes of socialisation, is "a multiplicity of realities rather than a single reality" (Hałas, 2007, p. 115). Identity attributes of leaders include predispositions indicative of awareness, judgement and action expressed by the motto "be, know, act". The motto can be the phrase: to be a leader you can trust is to make others around you respect you. The leadership framework in this aspect includes the following recommendations: "be" a professional, a person who is loyal to his/her organisation and who possesses good character traits, (such as honesty, competence, sincerity, commitment, integrity, courage, directness, imagination); "know" the four factors of leadership (follower, leader, communication, situation); yourself (your strengths and weaknesses, your knowledge and skills); human nature (human needs, emotions, stress reactions); your work (be professional and be able to train other people); your organisation (the climate and culture of the organisation, the unofficial leaders of the organisation), and "act", i.e. set direction (goal setting, problem solving, decision making, planning), implement (communication, coordination, supervision, evaluation), and motivate (developing morale, sense of community, advising, providing training) (Sharma & Jain, 2013, pp. 312–313).

In a similar vein, Bennis presented his reflection on grasping the differences between a manager and a leader. In his book *On Becoming a Leader*, the author created a list of differences, namely: (a) managers are administrators while leaders are innovators, (b) managers copy rules and apply them, while leaders formulate rules and regulations, (c) managers maintain the system and environment, while leaders develop the system and environment; (d) managers focus on the system and structure of the organisation, while leaders focus on people; (e) managers control the system to achieve goals, while leaders build trust to achieve the planned goals, (f) the manager's vision is shorter than the leader's vision; (g) a manager asks questions: "how and when?", while a leader asks: "what and why?") h) a manager follows rules and regulations, while a leader creates these rules and regulations; i) a manager accepts the status quo, while a leader questions it; j) a manager performs well, while a leader does things the right way. The above juxtaposition illustrating the differences between the distinguished constructs allows us to conclude that leadership is a broader term emphasising the importance of influencing other people to achieve desired goals, while a manager uses his or her power to motivate employees to perform their tasks (Mahmood, Muhammad & Bashir, 2012, p. 514).

When discussing the personality and identity aspect related to the discussed issue, it is worth clarifying that managerial and leadership careers as well as events and interactions in organisational situations lead to changes in definitions of self and others and to behaviours that protect identity (Blankenship, 1973, p. 88). It is impossible to overlook the clear references in these findings to Goffman's "identity policies practiced in interactions" (Hałas, 2007b, p. 148). In the managerial and leadership identity portrayed in this way, subjective reality consists of an 'internal world' that is accessible only to the person in question, and an 'external world' that is also accessible to other people and that forms the foundation of objective reality (Dawis, 2002, p. 428). The developmental impact of the interaction between an individual and the organisational environment is emphasised by S. Dill, Hilton and Retman among others, recognising that individuals develop through a series of interactions between themselves and the organisational environment (…) through the feedback and information that individuals get in response to their decisions and actions (Dalton, 2004, p. 95). Effective management and leardership are not not free of this dependency.

Agnieszka Cybal-Michalska

Final note:
Management for leadership? – educational implications

The quality of change in the contemporary world, to refer to the phrase coined by I. Wallerstein, "the world as we know it" (whereby, it is worth emphasising, the quality of social change in the author's vision is in fact even "the end of the world as we know it") (see Wallerstein, 2004, p. 55) contributes to changes in thinking about management. This leads to the observation that "for the first time in the history of mankind, a real chance has arisen for personal satisfaction and the freedom of initiative enjoyed by the direct inventors of ideas and things to become a condition for the proper functioning of their workplaces, and not merely the content of utopian, pro-humanist slogans" (Obuchowski, 2000). Indeed, as A. Giddens emphasises, a fundamental component underlying everyday activities of individuals is choice. Intellectual emancipation and the capacity for reflexive behaviour, in the world of permanent change and the diversity of social environments (in which the individual is directly and indirectly involved) enable the expression of personal subjectivity through the creation of individual lifestyles and the "choice" of identity (Whittington, 1992, pp. 695–696).

In this sense, the creation of management strategy and management style in the world oriented towards global change becomes not only a civilisational problem affecting the shape of organisational development, but also a problem having an individual dimension. Management is the most important part of any organisation and knowledge of management theory is the key element if we are to succeed in management, or leadership. This knowledge also applies to universities, which are after all organisations and no organisation can achieve its goals without effective management. For this reason, management is considered to be at the heart of any organisation (Mahmood, Muhammad & Bashir, 2012, p. 512).

The assumption of an inextricable link between leadership and management underpins the reflections in this chapter, emphasising that "leadership and management form patterns of complementary behaviours, actions, knowledge and skills. They should be seen on a continuum reflecting the performance of the managerial function, where the two categories, although related, are nonetheless distinct" (Michalak, 2014, p. 3). It is clear from the above that although management is associated with the ability to deal with complexity and leadership with change, as Kotter puts it, "once companies understand the fundamental difference between leadership and management, they can begin the process of training their best people to perform both roles simultaneously" (Kotter, 2005, pp. 119–120).

Many researchers are still contemplating the answer to the question of whether someone is born a leader or whether it is something that can be nurtured in oneself. Does the essence lie in innate charisma or in qualities that can be learned? (Bohoris & Vorria, 2007, p. 1). The answers, as one can infer from the considerations undertaken in this work, can be varied. The aspect which, due to the theme taken up in the final reflections, is worth dwelling on concerns the particular glorification of leadership. In the 1980s, researchers in the field of leadership and management advocated treating leadership as the antidote to all organisational failures. The "let's get rid of management" movement, which, as Kożusznik points out, was accompanied by the slogan: "people don't want to be managed, they want to be led" (Michalak, 2014, pp. 15–18) surprises with its radicality, but leads to thinking whether it is legitimate to direct the management process towards leadership.

Mintzberg, critical of putting the issue of leadership on a pedestal, who brings management to the fore, states that by treating leadership as "a function distinct from management, we are assigning an individual character to something that is social in nature. No matter how much we emphasise that the role of a leader is to empower or legitimise a group of employees, we are always thinking mainly of the person of a leader – every time we emphasise the issue of leadership, we belittle the group members and treat them merely as subordinates of the leader. In doing so, we also weaken the sense of community and group membership, so important in teamwork and essential in any organisation. Instead of focusing on leadership, we should be concerned with communities of human beings that naturally work together to achieve goals, and we should see leaders and managers as an integral part of these communities" (Mintzberg, 2013, pp. 26–27). In collaboration with managers at different levels, senior and more experienced managers set the goals of the organisation, and all those who work in the organisation make efforts to achieve these goals. Management is about creating the right context in the organisation to work effectively and also to help the organisation find its way among the opportunities and threats from the external environment. Managers at all levels shape the values and culture of the organisation through their decisions and by setting an example for others, however it is the experienced managers who usually have the clear and most direct influence. The achievements and successes of an organisation are the best evidence of the efforts and effective performance of managers (Darr, 2011, p. 8).

Contemporary organisations (and this also applies to universities) need both effective leaders and effective managers in order to be successful. This means task-oriented on the one hand, and innovation and visionary, on the other hand (Ricketts, 2009, p. 1).

The concepts of leadership and management have many similarities. Both involve influencing, working with other people and achieving goals (Ricketts, 2009, p. 2). The formation of the said dimensions requires an intentional and focused process of their development through education. Changing ideas about the nature of management and leadership, as well as challenges associated with traditional approaches to their development, have been a clear contributor to the emergence of many innovative trends in management and leadership education. Williams notes an increase in the demand for postgraduate and further education courses offered by universities. Hirsh and Carter note a clear shift towards more flexible and tailored training offerings to meet the requirements of individuals and organisations. Such a shift requires a reversal of many traditional educational priorities: from theory to practice, from parts to system, from stages and roles to processes, from knowledge to learning, from individual knowledge to partnership, and from analysis to reflective understanding. The basis for these changes can be traced to a paradigmatic shift marking a new quality of thinking about the nature of management and leadership and a change in philosophical perspectives on the role of management and leadership. The meta-reflection is mirrored in practice and refers to issues such as effective management and greater organisational competitiveness. Mole uses a clear distinction between the concepts of management training, education and development. In the theorist's view, *training* focuses on the employee's current work; *education* focuses on future work, while *development* focuses on the organisation. The contemporary trend focuses on education, but primarily on development. Development programmes prepare individuals to change and move in a new direction, which can be caused by transitions and developments in the organisation. Bush and Glover made a similar distinction when reviewing theories on leadership development, identifying three contrasting models of leadership development. Each of the distinctive approaches identifies the relative merits and weaknesses of respective ones. Each represents a significant philosophical perspective on the nature of management and leadership in organisations. The models highlighted are the as follows: "scientific" (technical) model, which relies on training to achieve clearly defined goals; the "humanistic" model focuses on people and strategically planned transformational interactions; and the "pragmatic" (rational) model, which focuses on projects, emphasising the urgent needs of individuals and groups. In order to better understand management education, Holman cites four recurring motifs in debates about the purpose, nature and value of higher education and adds a fifth element. In addition to the *epistemological* motif (reflecting assumptions about the nature of the knowledge sought) the *pedagogical* motif (referring to the nature of the learning process, intended outcomes and teaching methods) and the *organisational* motif (referring to the management and organisation of education) as well as the *social* motif (reflecting the role of education in society), he mentions *management*, thus referring to ideas about the nature of managerial practices. Referring to the diversity of the above motifs, it is not surprising that qualitatively different approaches to the topic of management and leadership development have emerged. In developing his approach, Holman identified four contemporary models of management education (see Table 1), concluding that academic liberalism (important because of its over-reliance on theory) and practical vocational training (important because of its over-reliance on action) are desirable if we are to develop practice-oriented managers. Furthermore, Holman proposes that it is empirical liberalism and empirical/critical approaches that shape managers who will be able to meet prospective change and the needs of organisations and society. Empirical pedagogy promotes learning and development in the natural environment at work and points to the ability to deal with the complex nature of actual management practices.

Table 1. "Contemporary Models of Management Education" (version, after: Bolden, 2007, p. 4)

Academic liberalism	It assumes that management education should be primarily concerned with following objective management knowledge. In doing so, this approach seeks to spread general principles and theories that can be applied in a relatively scientific and rational way. From this perspective, the aim of management development should be to produce a "management scholar" who is able to analyse and apply theoretical principles. The main teaching methods are lectures, seminars, case studies and experiments.
Empirical liberalism	It has similar assumptions to academic liberalism, but pays more attention to a practical approach that is a result of managerial experience rather than theoretical and cognitive practices. The main aim of this approach is to create a "thinking practitioner", equipped with relevant practical skills and knowledge and the ability to adapt and learn from given situations. The main teaching methods are group work, hands-on learning and self-development.
Empirical professional training	It stems from economic and organisational concerns to equip managers with the right skills and knowledge required by the organisation and this is the role of management education. The aim of this approach is to educate a "competent manager", equipped with the necessary interpersonal and technical competences required by organisations.

Critical/ empirical approach	It aims, as Holman emphasises, to liberate managers and other organisational employees from oppression and alienation. In such a sense, this approach has much in common with empirical liberalism although it calls for a more critical level of reflection that enables individuals to become more insightful in terms of their knowledge and the quality of their actions also in order to formulate practical and emancipatory forms of action. Hence, the main focus of this approach is to educate a "critical practitioner" able to face and develop new ways of acting. The main teaching methods are approaches that are based on critical hands-on learning and critical reflection.

In the context of the ponderings about the purpose of education in the subject of management and leadership, there is a clear trend to move away from traditional formal programmes towards flexible and empirical initiatives. Weindling noted that surprisingly few programmes are based on explicit management theories and leadership practices. Hirsch and Carter, in turn, note three important tensions with which management educators must confront. Firstly, with the segmentation of formal programmes, there is increasing pressure to make learning curricula adaptable and relevant to leaders and managers at every level of the organisation. Secondly, the rise of personalised learning such as coaching and 360-degree assessments poses a major challenge, due to temporal considerations, more time is needed to tailor and support a specific provision. Thirdly, with the disappearance of traditional career structures and lifetime employment, managers receive little support in terms of long-term career planning. Hence, it is noticeable that there are a number of factors that influence the current range and dimension of management and leadership. Some of these are directly related to the quality and development of management education. Others are conceptual in nature and relate to the assumptions, goals of education, the nature of management and leadership and the relative nature of the individual – group relationship. Each of these issues has a high degree of complexity, but without an awareness of the underlying issues behind the assumptions, it will be difficult to choose an effective approach to leadership development (Bolden, 2007, pp. 2–5)[7] including management for leadership.

The number of developmental and educational initiatives brings to mind a reflection on the organisational dimension of education. Gosling and Mintzberg have proposed seven main assumptions on which true management should be based. Addressing the issue of management education, the researchers point out the following: a) management education should be limited to practising man-

---

[7] The importance of the truth that you reap what you sow is highlighted, giving as an example the situation that if the development and reward system favours the contribution of an individual rather than the involvement of the collective, then it will be difficult to create a culture that encourages collaboration and shared leadership.

agers, selected on the basis of their effectiveness; b) management education and practice should run in parallel and should be integrated; c) management education should draw on work and life experience; d) prudent reflection is key in management education; e) management development should result in organisational development; f) management education should be an interactive process; g) every dimension of education should facilitate learning. The implications of the principles highlighted are manifold for both those who participate in management and leadership development and those who create and deliver educational offer. The interplay between experience, theory, practice and reflection, between the development of the individual and the development of the organisation, and between the provider of the offer and the attendee deserves special attention. The phenomenon of management can be viewed from a number of perspectives, and each assumes a processual character. The phenomenon of leadership is viewed in a similar way (leadership is not something you teach or learn – it is a process of acquiring knowledge). The processual context allows for the possibility of creating actions to manage one's career and monitor one's career for leadership. The distinguished approach points to the new quality of partnerships between companies and management or business schools, which will enrich the discourse on managing organisational development on both sides. In this sense, leadership development, especially the opportunity to step back and take a fresh look at practice, should be part and parcel of all aspects of organisational performance and therefore, organisational management. In order to make sure that one gets the most out of leadership development, it is recommended to critically evaluate the current concepts of leadership and learning within one's organisation, to think about the developmental needs of both individuals and organisations, and to diagnose how these needs are changing given the temporal dynamics. This also means recognising various options and development offers from different knowledge providers and negotiating the match between teaching curricula and students' requirements in order to maximise the benefits of learning and the transfer of acquired knowledge to the workplace. The quality of the management processes preceding and following educational and development activities is a predictor of whether newly acquired competences will be valued and put into practice. It is not insignificant to look at other organisational systems and processes, especially HR strategy. The individual perspective also mandates allowing oneself the "inner voice" and recognising and working through psychological barriers to effective leadership, such as low self-esteem, lack of confidence, fear of failure or rejection, cognitive "narrowing" and the negative effects of stress. Dealing with the problems highlighted above involves using techniques such as reinforcement, psychological reconstruction, and social skills improvement. It is recommended to build on strengths and look for ways to deal with weaknesses. The key to success in being a leader is not to fill gaps in competence, but to reinforce your strengths and uniqueness within oneself. Gosling and Murphy talk about the importance of continuity in the process of change. The sense of Self continuity, despite the passage of time, is one of the most important identity components regarding an individual subject. Transformative changes may occur, but in most cases, the situation requires a considered approach and the use of internalised individual and organisational skills. The importance, role and influence of organisational culture and context in encouraging, motivating and inspiring people to work in a particular job by using an appropriate communication style to present its goals and values is emphasised. The topic of leadership and organisational development needs to be viewed in the long term, realising its processual nature. In this context, it is worth considering how different learning and development activities fit into the life and career course of individuals and organisations (Bolden, 2007, pp. 9–11).

The ponderings on the crystallisation of leader identity are testament to the value of the educational leadership debate. The main categories belonging to this grounded theory include different stages of leader identity. The process of developing leader identity means going through stages of development in contact with a group that changes one's view of oneself, of others, and broadens one's perspective on leadership. The following stages of leader's identity development are illustrated by proponents of developmental influences based on empirical research: awareness, exploration (engagement), leader identified, diverse leadership, generativity, integration (synthesis). The first stage involves noticing that leaders exist. The second stage is a time of purposeful engagement, group experience and the exercise of responsibility. This is a phase of skill development, including observation of leadership models. In the third stage, participants realise that groups are made up of leaders and followers. At this stage, one leader emerges, i.e. *the* leader and he or she is responsible for the group's performance. At the fourth stage, the perception of the positional leader's role takes place, as an entity that connects the community and shapes the group culture. At the fifth stage, leadership activity is experienced and the drive for change, interconnectedness, acceptance of responsibility and concern for the development of others can be seen. The final stage is active engagement in leadership. Seeing leadership as a day-to-day process, as an identity dimension of an individual with self-confidence, striving for congruence and internal integrity. The leader understands the complexity of the organisation and demonstrates systemic thinking. Investment in leadership, internalised as a personality trait, makes the leader cognitively flexible and able to apply their knowledge and skills in new contexts. Seeing leadership as an everyday experience (Komives et al., 2005, pp. 605–607).

A cognitively interesting context for reflectively addressing the question posed in the endnote is illustrated by Fenton's view, i.e. leaders stand out because they are different. They question assumptions and are suspicious of tradition. They seek the truth and make decisions based on facts rather than preconceptions. They prefer innovation (Bhamani, Rose & Bramble, 2012, p. 14). If we assume that the author was referring only to leaders in his opinion, then by the same token, it would have to be concluded that managers are not necessarily truth-seeking and innovative, but they are happy to stick to tradition. The spirit of the times does not allow us to simplify this much. When discussing the conditions necessary for a manager to become an inspirer of change, Seiling mentions the qualities that can be attributed to a leader. These include skills in areas such as: "seeing a different reality, expressing the unspoken, challenging, and taking the enormous risk of being perceived as lacking in realism – or even lacking in credibility – because of a desire to create an entirely new working environment" (Brown, 2006, pp. 45–48). The complexity of the determinants of leadership and management is therefore applicable to new ideas and trends indicating the relational nature of the constructs discussed in this work.

Bibliography

Bhamani, M., Rose, T., & Bramble, L. (2012). *The difference between leadership and management schools of thought.* Athabasca: Athabasca University.
Blanchard, K. (2010). *Przywództwo wyższego stopnia.* Warszawa: Wydawnictwo Naukowe PWN.
Blanchard, K.H., & Hersey, P. (1996). Great ideas. Life cycle theory of leadership. *Training and Development Journal, 23*(5), 26-34.
Blankenship, R.L. (1973). Organizational careers: an interactionist perspective. *The Sociological Quarterly, 14*(1), 88-98.
Bobzien, M. (2002). Auf dem Weg zur lernenden Gemeinschaft: Empowerment und Qualitätsmanagement. Hilfreiche Orientierungen im Dreiecksverhältnis öffentliche Verwaltung, Einrichtungen und Nutzer Innen. In A. Lenz, & W. Stark (Eds.), *Empowerment. Neue Perspektiven für psychosoziale Praxis und Organisation.* Tübingen: DGVT Verlag.
Bohoris, G.A., & Vorria, E.P. (2007). Leadership vs management. Business excellence/performance management view. [Linköping Electronic Conference Proceedings]. http://www.ep.liu.se/ecp/026/076/ecp0726076.pdf (accessed on 20.01.2024).
Bolden, R. (2007). Trends and perspectives in management and leadership development. *Business Leadership Review, IV,* 2-5.
Brilman, J., & Bolesta-Kukułka K. (2002). *Nowoczesne koncepcje i metody zarządzania.* Warszawa: Polskie Wydawnictwo Ekonomiczne.
Brown, T. (2006). Nowy rodzaj pracownika wymaga nowego rodzaju menedżera. In J. Biolos (Ed.), *Zarządzanie karierą.* Warszawa: Studio Emka Harvard Business School Press.
Bugdol, M. (2006). *Wartości organizacyjne. Szkice z teorii organizacji i zarządzania.* Kraków: Wydawnictwo Uniwersytetu Jagiellońskiego.
Bush, T. (2011). *Theories of educational leadership and management.* London: Sage.
Cervinkova, H. (2012). Badania w działaniu i zaangażowana antropologia edukacyjna. *Teraźniejszość – Człowiek – Edukacja, 1*(57), 7-18.
Cheng, Y-C. (2024). A typology of multiple school leadership. *Education Sciences, 14*(1), 70, https://doi.org/10.3390/educsci14010070.
Cho, T., & Faerman, S.R. (2010). An integrative approach to empowerment. Construct definition, measurement, and validation. *Public Management Review, 12*(1), pp. 33-51.

Conger, J.A., & Kanungo, R.N. (1988). The empowerment process: integrating theory and practice. *Academy of Management Review*, *13*(3), 471–482.

Dalton, G.W. (2004). Developmental views of careers in organizations. In M.B. Arthur, D.T. Hall, & B.P. Lawrence (Eds.). *Handbook of Career Theory*. Cambridge: Cambridge University Press, pp. 89–109.

Darr, K. (2011). Introduction to management and leadership concepts, principles and practices. In R.E. Burke, & L.H. Friedman (Eds.), *Essentials of management and leadership in public health*. Sudbury, MA: Jones and Bartlett Publishers, pp. 7–22.

Dawis, R.V. (2002). Person-environment-correspondence theory. In D. Brown (Ed.), *Career choice and development*. San Francisco: Jossey-Bass, pp. 427–464.

De Toni, A.F., & De Marchi, S. (2023). *Self-organized schools. Educational leadership and innovative learning environments*. New York and London: Routledge.

Domański, H. (2019). Stratyfikacyjne funkcje prestiżu. *Przegląd Socjologiczny*, *68*(2), 187–208.

Dorczak, R. (2012). Modele współpracy szkoły z organizacjami w środowisku lokalnym. In G. Mazurkiewicz (Ed.), *Jakość edukacji: różnorodne perspektywy*. Kraków: Wydawnictwo Uniwersytetu Jagiellońskiego, pp. 311–331.

Döbert, H. (2011). Monitorowanie oświaty w Niemczech: strategie i problemy. In M.S. Szymański (Ed.). *Polityka i badania oświatowe w Niemczech i Polsce*. Warszawa: Wydawnictwo Akademickie "Żak".

Dryll, E. (2021). Characteristic of the school environment. In G. Katra, & E. Sokołowska (Eds.). *The role and tasks of psychologist in a contemporary school*. Warszawa: Wydawnictwa Uniwersytetu Warszawskiego, pp. 34–46.

Fisiak, J. (Ed.) (2003). *Nowy słownik Fundacji Kościuszkowskiej angielsko-polski*. New York, Kraków: Kościuszko Foundation, "Universitas".

Framework of Reference. The Making of: Leadership in Education. A European Qualification Network for Effective School Leadership, 2011, http://www.leadership-in education.eu/fileadmin/Framework/EN_Framework.pdf (accessed on 8.08.2014)

Fullan, M. (2020). The nature of leadership is changing. *European Journal of Education*, *55* (2), 139–142. https://doi.org/10.1111/ejed.12388.

Garbarski, L., Rutkowski, I., & Wrzosek, W. (2000). *Marketing. Punkt zwrotny nowoczesnej firmy*. Warszawa: Polskie Wydawnictwo Ekonomiczne.

Gierszewska, G., & Romanowska, M. (2002). *Analiza strategiczna przedsiębiorstwa*. Warszawa: Polskie Wydawnictwo Ekonomiczne.

Griffin, R.W. (1996). *Podstawy zarządzania organizacjami*. Warszawa: Wydawnictwo Naukowe PWN.

Griffin, R.W. (2004). *Podstawy zarządzania organizacjami*. Warszawa: Wydawnictwo Naukowe PWN.

Griffin, R.W. (2021). *Podstawy zarządzania organizacjami*. Warszawa: Wydawnictwo Naukowe PWN.

Hackman, J.R., & Morris, C.G. (1975). Group tasks, group interaction process, and group performance effectiveness: a review and proposed integration. *Advances in Experimental Social Psychology*, *8*, 45–99, https://doi.org/10.1016/S0065-2601(08)60248-8.

Hall, H. (2007). *Marketing w szkolnictwie*. Warszawa: Wolters Kluwer Polska.

Hallinger, P. (2010). Developing instructional leadership. In B. Davies, & M. Brundrett (Eds.), *Developing Successful Leadership*. Dordrecht: Springer, pp. 61–76.

Hallinger, H., & Heck, R. (1996). Reassessing the principal's role in school effectiveness: A review of empirical research, 1980–1995. *Educational Administration Quarterly, 32*(1), 5–44.

Hallinger, P., & Murphy, J. (1985). Assessing the instructional leadership behaviour of principal. *Elementary School Journal, 86*(2), 217–248.

Hałas, E. (1998). Interakcjonizm symboliczny. In A. Kojder (Ed.), *Encyklopedia socjologii*, vol. 1. Warszawa: Oficyna Naukowa.

Hałas, E. (2007a). *Symbole i społeczeństwo. Szkice z socjologii interpretacyjnej*. Warszawa: Wydawnictwa Uniwersytetu Warszawskiego.

Hałas, E. (2007b). Osobliwości interakcjonizmu Ervinga Goffmana. *Studia Socjologiczne, 184*(1), 147–161.

Harris, A., & Jones, M. (2023). The importance of school leadership? What we know. *School Leadership & Management, 43*(5), 449–453, https://doi.org/10.1080/13632434.2023.2287806.

Hernik, K., Solon-Lipiński, M., & Stasiowski, J. (2012). *Współpraca szkół z podmiotami zewnętrznymi. Raport z badania otoczenia instytucjonalnego przedszkoli, szkół podstawowych i gimnazjów*. Warszawa: Instytut Badań Edukacyjnych.

Herriger, N. (2002). *Empowerment in der Sozialen Arbeit*. Stuttgart, Berlin, Köln: Kohlhammer.

Huxham, C. (2003). Theorizing collaboration practice. *Public Management Review, 5*(3), 401–423.

Huxham, C., & Beech, P. (2008). Inter-organizational power. In S. Cropper, M. Ebers, & C. Huxham (Eds.), *The Oxford handbook of inter-organizational relations*. New York: Oxford University Press.

Huxham, C., & Vangen, P. (2000). Leadership in the shaping and implementation of collaboration agendas: how things happen in a (not quite) joined-up world. Special Forum on Managing in the New Millennium. *Academy of Management Journal, 43*(6), 1159–1175.

Jacobson, S.L. (2005). The recruitment and retention of school leaders: understanding administrator supply and demand. In N. Bascia et al. (Eds.), *International Handbook of Educational Policy*. Dordrecht: Springer, pp. 457–470.

Katz, D., & Kahn, R.L. (1979). *Społeczna psychologia organizacji*, Warszawa: PWN.

Kilian, P. (2007). *The ABC effective leadership: A practical overview of evidence based leadership theory*. Melbourne: Australian Leadership Development Center.

Komives, P.R. et al. (2005). Developing a leadership identity: a grounded theory. *Journal of Student Development, 46*(6), 605–607.

Kotter, J.P. (2005). Co właściwie robią przywódcy. Harvard Business Review Polska, no. 28.

Kreisberg, S. (1992). *Transforming power. Domination, empowerment and education*. Albany: State University of New York Press.

Kwiatkowski, S.M. (2011). Typologie przywództwa. In S.M. Kwiatkowski, J.M. Michalak, & I. Nowosad (Eds.), *Przywództwo edukacyjne w szkole i jej otoczeniu*. Warszawa: Difin, pp. 13–22.

Lawson, T. (2011). Empowerment in education: liberation, governance or a distraction? A Review. *Power and Education, 3*(2). https://doi.org/10.2304/power.2011.3.2.89.

Mabey, C., & Finch-Lees, T. (2008). *Management and leadership development*. London: Sage.

Mahmood, Z., Muhammad, B., & Bashir, Z. (2012). Review of classical management theories. *International Journal of Social Sciences and Education*, 2(1), 512–522.
Manterys, A., & Mucha, J. (2009). Nowe perspektywy teorii socjologicznej. Punkt widzenia 2009 r. In A. Manterys, & J. Mucha (Eds.), *Nowe perspektywy teorii socjologicznej*. Kraków: Zakład Wydawniczy "Nomos", pp. VII–XXVII.
Marshall, G. (2005). *Słownik socjologii i nauk społecznych*. Warszawa: Wydawnictwo Naukowe PWN.
Maxwell, J.C. (2010). *Etyka*. Warszawa: Emka.
Mazurkiewicz, G. (2011). Przywództwo dla uczenia się. Jak wyjść poza schemat? In S.M. Kwiatkowski, J.M. Michalak, & I. Nowosad (eds.), *Przywództwo edukacyjne w szkole i jej otoczeniu*. Warszawa: Difin, pp. 23–39.
McDonnell, L.M. (2009). A political science perspective on educational policy analysis. In G. Sykes, B. Schneider, & D.N. Plank (Eds.), *Handbook of education policy research*. New York: Routledge, https://doi.org/10.4324/9780203880968.
Michalak, J.M. (2010). Przywództwo dla wzmacniania szans edukacyjnych uczniów. In I. Nowosad, I. Mortag, & J. Ondrakova (Eds.), *Jakość życia i jakość szkoły. Wprowadzenie w zagadnienia jakości i efektywności pracy szkoły*. Zielona Góra: Oficyna Wydawnicza Uniwersytetu Zielonogórskiego.
Michalak M.J. (2014). *Przywództwo w zarządzaniu szkołą*. Raport Ośrodka Rozwoju Edukacji, http://www.bc.ore.edu.pl/Content/618/przywodztwo_w_zarzadzaniu_szkola.pdf (accessed on 8.08.2014).
Mintzberg, H. (2013). *Zarządzanie*. Warszawa: Nieoczywiste.
Misztal, B. (2000). *Teoria socjologiczna a praktyka społeczna*. Kraków: Universitas.
Moczydłowska, J.M. (2013). Empowerment – upodmiotowienie we wspólnocie. *Ekonomika i Organizacja Przedsiębiorstwa*, 11, 15–23.
Nalaskowski, A. (2001). *Przestrzenie i miejsca szkoły*. Kraków: Oficyna Wydawnicza "Impuls".
Nowak, S. (1970). *Metodologia badań socjologicznych*. Warszawa: PWN.
Obuchowski, K. (2000). *Człowiek intencjonalny, czyli o tym, jak być sobą*. Poznań: Dom Wydawniczy "Rebis".
Paluchowski, W.J. (2007). *Diagnoza psychologiczna: proces, narzędzia, standardy*. Warszawa: Wydawnictwa Akademickie i Profesjonalne.
Patton, W., & McMahon, M. (2006). *Career development and systems theory. Connecting theory and practice*. Rotterdam: Brill.
Pluta-Olearnik, M. (2006). *Rozwój usług edukacyjnych w erze społeczeństwa informacyjnego*. Warszawa: Polskie Wydawnictwo Ekonomiczne.
Professional Standards for Educational Leaders (2015). Reston, VA: National Policy Board for Educational Administration, https://www.npbea.org/psel/.
Przyszczypkowski, K., & Solarczyk-Ambrozik, E. (2002). *Strategia rozwoju oświaty w województwie wielkopolskim*. Poznań: Sejmik Województwa Wielkopolskiego.
Pyżalski, J. (2014). *Kompetencje przywódcze dyrektorów szkół i placówek w krajach Unii Europejskiej i Stanach Zjednoczonych*. Warszawa: Ośrodek Rozwoju Edukacji.
Ricketts, K.G. (2009). Leadership vs management. In *Leadership Behavior*. Lexington, KY: Cooperative Extension Service, University of Kentucky College of Agriculture, http://www2.ca.uky.edu/agc/pubs/elk1/elk1103/elk1103.pdf (accessed on 20.01.2024).

Rokicka, E. (1992). Pojęcie "kariery". Perspektywa strukturalno-funkcjonalna i interakcjonistyczna. *Przegląd Socjologiczny*, *41*, 115–121.

Rosalska, M. (2006). Empowerment w kształceniu ustawicznym. *E-mentor* 3(15), www.e-mentor.edu.pl/artykul/index/numer/15/id/305 (accessed on 8.08.2014).

Rothstein, R.L. (1995). The empowerment effort that come undone. *Harvard Bussines Review*, *73*(1).

Scott, J., & Marshall, G. (2009). *A dictionary of sociology*. Oxford: Oxford University Press.

Seliga, R., & Woźniak, A. (2014). Istota marketingu relacji. In M. Al.-Noorachi (Ed.), *Współczesne wyzwania marketingowe – wybrane zagadnienia*. Łódź, Warszawa: Wydawnictwo Społecznej Akademii Nauk, pp. 235–275.

Shani, D., & Chalasani, P. (1992). Exploiting niches using relationship marketing. *Journal of Consumer Marketing*, *9*(3), 33–42.

Sharma, M.K., & Jain, P. (2013). Leadership management: principles, models and theories. *Global Journal of Management and Business Studies*, *3*(3), 309–318.

Smith, J. (2006). *Empowerment. Jak zwiększać zaangażowanie pracowników*. Gliwice: Helion.

Smith, R.D. (2021). *Strategic planning for public relation*. 6th ed. London: Routledge.

Smykowski, B. (1996). Ludzie i ich liderzy. In A. Brzezińska, & A. Potok (Eds.), *Kształcenie liderów społeczności wiejskich*. Poznań: Fundusz Współpracy, pp. 53–68.

Solomon, B.B. (1976). *Black empowerment. Social work in oppressed communities*. New York: Columbia University Press.

Stimmer, F. (2000). *Grundlagen des Methodischen Handelns in der Sozialen Arbeit*. Stuttgart: Kohlhammer.

Stoner, J.A.F, Freeman, R.E, & Gilbert, D.E. (2001). *Kierowanie*. Warszawa: Polskie Wydawnictwo Ekonomiczne.

Surej, P.J., & De Villiers, R. (2022). Factors affecting the success of marketing in higher education: a relationship marketing perspective. *Journal of Marketing for Higher Education*, *8*, 1–20.

Szmagalski, J. (1994). O "budzeniu sił ludzkich" nie po polsku: Koncepcje "empowerment" w anglojęzycznej literaturze z zakresu edukacji i pracy socjalnej. *Kwartalnik Pedagogiczny*, *3*, 113–128.

Tengland, P.-A. (2008). Empowerment: a conceptual discussion. *Health Care Analysis*, *16* (2), 77–96.

Wallerstein, I. (2004). *Koniec świata jaki znamy*. Warszawa: Wydawnictwo Naukowe "Scholar".

Whittington, R. (1992). Putting Giddens into action: social system and managerial agency. *Journal of Management Studies*, *29*(6), 693–712.

Ziółkowski, M. (2006). Teoria socjologiczna początku XXI wieku. In A. Jasińska-Kania (Ed.). *Współczesne teorie socjologiczne*, vol. 1. Warszawa: Wydawnictwo Naukowe "Scholar".

Żuk, G. (2016). *Edukacja aksjologiczna. Zarys problematyki*. Lublin: Wydawnictwo UMCS.

Summary

The leadership issues addressed in this publication were also analysed in relation to educational practices. As the proposed analyses have shown, theoretical assumptions from the field of management and leadership have a direct bearing on daily practices implemented by school leaders. Given that management theory and practice is a dynamically developing field, it can be assumed that thinking about management of school as an organisation and the processes carried out in it will also be subject to development.

However, it is hard to agree with the that it is possible to directly translate leadership and management concepts into the educational context. The specific nature of the objectives, the axiological aspect, the multiplicity of stakeholders interested in influencing the direction and dynamics of the processes carried out in schools, mean that being a leader in an educational context requires more than just leadership competences. Furthermore, the diversity and complexity of leadership concepts makes it legitimate to raise questions about the role of leaders' individual preferences in the choice of management and leadership strategies, about the ways in which power is exercised or shared in schools, about the possibilities of developing principals' leadership competences not only at the stage of gaining authority and qualifications to lead schools, but also as part of lifelong education.

A school community leader is more than an efficient manager. It is a person who integrates many roles in their activities. In addition to the typical leadership roles, they also perform educational and upbringing tasks. An effective principal is able to tap into their own resources and those of their environment. They are able to manage, direct and control and, at the same time, understand the processes they conduct and are able to facilitate them. However, competences related to leadership can be considered an extremely important component of the professional profile of a school principal or a director of another educational institution. It is this area of competence that determines the effectiveness of their actions, the quality of their relationships, and their capacity to implement theoretical assumptions about the school's mission and vision into their daily practices. That is why it is so crucial to adequately diagnose and develop actual rather than only declarative competence resources of educational leaders. Bearing in mind that knowledge development in this area may not be sufficient and may not be directly transferable to specific leadership and management skills, it becomes important to create opportunities to develop and review specific skills related to leading, sharing power, controlling, motivating and building relationships with the school's immediate and distant social environment.

The aim of this publication was not only to identify current themes in the discussion on the role of leadership in education and educational leadership. Reference to dominant theories, both general and those relating to educational contexts, may be helpful in reflecting on the direction and scope of leadership training for education. The themes presented can be inspiring for designers of training offers for school leaders at different stages of their professional careers and can benefit leaders developing their professional development through self-education and self-reflection.